Gary Elson and Oliver Lucanus

Gouramis
and Other
Labyrinth
Fishes

Everything About Natural History, Purchase,
Health Care, Breeding, and Species Identification

Filled with Full-color Photographs
and Illustrations

BARRON'S

CONTENTS

GOURAMI BASICS

In the modern aquarium hobby, Labyrinth Fishes get no respect. People think they know these longtime favorites too well and that these fascinating fish are all the same. As with most things connected with water, once one goes below the surface, nothing could be further from the truth.

An Intriguing Assortment

The fish the hobby refers to as *Gouramis* (more properly Anabantoids or Labyrinth Fishes) offer an astonishing range of body shapes, sizes, and lifestyles. Diversity always attracts people who wish to learn about their fish, and Anabantoids have a lot to offer. The pikelike *Luciocephalus pulcher,* a relentlessly efficient stealth predator, seems a world away from the small, gentle Dwarf and Honey Gouramis. When looking at tiny 1.5-inch (3-cm) Licorice Gouramis (*Parosphromenus* sp.), how could the uninitiated expect them to be in the same relatively small group as the popular, food fish–sized Giant and Kissing Gouramis, which can weigh in at several pounds?

The Five Labyrinth Fish Groups Described in This Manual
✔ Osphroneminae—Gouramis
✔ Sphaerichthyinae—The Chocolate Gouramis
✔ Macropodinae—Paradise Fish and Combtails

Chocolate Gouramis (Sphaerichthys sp.) are found in slow-moving streams such as this.

✔ Ctenopinae—Bettas, Trichopsis, and Ctenops
✔ Anabantinae—Bush Fish, Climbing Perch, Kissers

The relationship between aquarists and these fish goes back to the very beginnings of the indoor fish-keeping hobby. Imagine the excitement of a nineteenth-century aquarist seeing a small, vividly colored fish and knowing it could not only survive but prosper and maybe even breed under the primitive fishbowl conditions that could be offered to it. The Labyrinth Fishes of Asia, carefully carried to Europe or the Americas in tin containers by sailors, must have appeared very exotic indeed. The then-popular Paradise Fish from Southern Asia (and their *Ctenopoma* relatives from Africa) had everything going for them in the early days of the aquarium trade. They are tolerant to cool water, display lovely colors, have attractive body shapes, display interesting and peaceful behaviors, and have very intriguing breeding strategies. Although changes in technology and equipment have made fish keeping easier, both for humans and for the fish, Gouramis and their relatives have retained their central place

The Labyrinth Organ

The labyrinth organ may work a bit like a lung, but it is an entirely different solution to the problem of how to remove oxygen from air. The gill, a fish's usual breathing apparatus, is modified in a Labyrinth Fish. An extension to the gill branch is located inside the fish, in a cavity above the gill cover. It is an extremely convoluted, moist structure that allows the fish to use atmospheric air. The labyrinth organ is an effective adaptation to low-oxygen habitats.

in the pet shops of the world. Once an individual factors in their toughness, the fact they breathe surface air, and their ability to flourish in community aquariums, it is no wonder a number of Gouramis are the bread-and-butter fish of the trade.

Among those who take the time to learn, familiarity has never bred contempt with these animals. The more aquarists learn about them, the more they find surprises. Labyrinth Fishes have plenty to offer to those who like to study life off the beaten track. The well-known, readily available species are great fish. The newly discovered species are showing some really unexpected features that make them well worth the trouble to find them. Who could ask for anything more?

Distribution

Water and air: Labyrinth Fishes are defined by their relation to air almost as much as to water. They can breathe atmospheric oxygen at the surface with their labyrinth organ while retaining the ability to remove oxygen from water via their gills. The degree to which they will use their labyrinth organ differs from species to species. To understand how this works, one has to look at where Labyrinth Fishes come from.

Geography: The approximately 115 scientifically described species of Gouramis and their relatives live in a broad band across Southeast Asia and Africa, with introduced populations in the Caribbean, Madagascar, South and Central America, and the southern United States. As a definable group, they are relatively recent, at about 50 million years ago in the fossil record. Their habitats can vary considerably, as can their sizes and body shapes. On a recent trip to Southeast Asia, the authors encountered Gouramis in various types of habitats, as described below.

Not far from the island city of Singapore, in the southern Malaysian province of Johor, none of the original forest was left. All waterways seemed to have been adapted and modified for human needs,

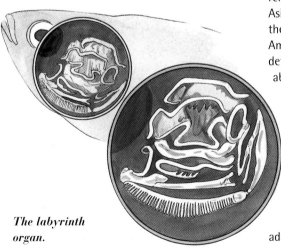

The labyrinth organ.

Distribution of Anabantoid species.

especially for the immense palm oil plantations. This industry seemed to have turned every water course into a drainage or irrigation ditch to one degree or another.

The banks of the smaller streams were lined with papyrus and oil palm trees, which provided a fair degree of cooling shade. The water was clear and had many low-light aquatic ferns growing in it. Still, areas of the shaded streams yielded lots of halfbeak live-bearers and small, attractive, brightly blue-eyed Pygmy Croaking Gouramis *(Trichopsis pumila)*. Where the water had overflowed the banks and formed swamps among the trees seemed to be bubble nests approximately every 3 feet (1 m) or so. The Blue Gourami, *Trichogaster trichopterus,* was found nesting in large numbers there. The same adaptable Gourami was also found close by feeding in faster-flowing waters that it shared with several barb species.

Close to Kuala Lumpur, a once-natural pond turned pig farm reservoir yielded more than a nasty odor. Giant Gouramis *(Osphronemus goramy)* are often kept on pig farms. Their willingness to eat nutrient-rich pig manure makes these food fish very popular with farmers, who use them as the first stage in a primitive manure-recycling process. The pond in question, lined on one side by a banana plantation, was very polluted and foul smelling. The surface was covered in water hyacinth *(Eichhornia crassipes)*—a popular water garden and backyard pond plant. Giant Gouramis reaching 2 feet (0.6 m) long congregated around the farm's waste outlet pipes. The shallower plant-choked margins featured nesting Blue Gouramis, probably the once-clean pond's original inhabitants.

While this sort of scenario falls well into the "don't try this at home" range, it does show the basic toughness of these fish. As bacteria feed on decomposing wastes, they can consume most of the oxygen in water. The fact that Gouramis can be observed prospering in such an unlikely habitat shows how their labyrinth air-breathing organ allows them to adapt to extreme wild conditions. Seeing how this ability transfers to often overcrowded home aquariums is not hard. Not all Gouramis use their labyrinth organs to the same degree. However, the more popular types usually breathe at the surface.

A key difference between the popular aquarium Gouramis and their more difficult-to-keep cousins is this adaptation. Scientists speculate that these fish evolved this ability in response to the challenge of surviving in hot, plant-choked, low-oxygen waters. However, this ability has stood them in good stead as human expansion has forever altered their original habitats. Various species of popular Gouramis can be found not only on pig farms but also in rice paddies, highway and city ditches, and other less-than-pristine waterways.

Water Quality

If some popular Gouramis coexist well with humans and their farms in the wild, others are much more challenging aquarium inhabitants. Almost every tropical aquatic environment offers variations on two types of water: the so-called white- or clear-water and black-water habitats.

White water has nothing to do with rapids. This water is of low-to-medium hardness and slightly cloudy if held up in a glass. Its chemical composition is not very different from tap water. Even if a local water source is naturally soft and acidic, most water companies will raise the pH to protect pipes from slow corrosion caused by natural acidity. Most easily available Gouramis and Anabantoids prosper in such mineral- and nutrient-rich water.

Black water occurs in most forest areas due to a combination of heavy rain and decomposing leaves and wood. Peat bogs and most freshwater bogs have tea-colored black water, characterized by a low mineral content but a lot of tannins in the water. The water is very acidic, and the acids in the water render it low in bacteria. The low mineral content of the water forces fish to develop differently structured eggs and finely tuned metabolisms. Many black-water fish, be they Asian Gouramis, South American Tetras, African Dwarf Cichlids, or North American Dace, can adapt to living in clean water of medium hardness. However, they will always be susceptible to bacterial illness and will often be unable to reproduce outside of their natural conditions.

Water Chemistry

Water hardness is the measure of dissolved minerals in a water supply. Although aquarium books will use a variety of measures (German degrees of hardness, the French system, and others), most hobbyist test kits will simply measure parts per million (ppm). Fish from mineral-poor water are accustomed to very low ppm counts and may indeed have evolved a need for such conditions.

Aquarium test kits do not measure all qualities of hardness. An advanced aquarist or fish breeder should acquire an electronic meter to measure electrical conductivity (a more accurate measure of the minerals in water).

Gouramis are often found in swamps, like this Croaking Gourami (**Trichopsis pumila**) *habitat.*

Understanding minerals in water becomes a hobby in itself for those interested in chemistry. Those who simply want to keep fish should look into the composition of their local water supply and choose fish that can live within the parameters offered.

The pH of water is another cause of confusion in the hobby. In aquarist's terms, it is the measure of the acidity or alkalinity of water. A pH of 7.0 is neutral—lower is more acidic, higher is more alkaline. It is not a finely graded scale. The differences between a pH of 7.0 and 6.0 are immense. Aquarium fish can come from water at a range between pH 4.0 and 9.5, with the great majority coming from between pH 6.0 and 8.0.

Gouramis, like other rain forest fish, often need more acidic water. Many water acidification products are available in aquarium stores, but they should be used with great care. Buffering is a key concept in aquarium water management. The term refers to the ability of the mineral content of water to neutralize acids. If acidifying aquarium products are added to well-buffered water, the drop in pH will quickly be neutralized, and the pH will rapidly bounce back to its original level (or close). Such bounces in pH are extremely dangerous to fish.

Before using any of these acids, the aquarist must test them on water with no fish in it. In general, using them is a bad idea. They require the aquarist to constantly monitor water quality, especially during the all-important water changes. Keeping black-water Gouramis (since they are small) in purchased reverse osmosis water mixed with tap water would be easier than modifying water with chemicals. Unbuffered water, such as rainwater or pure water from a reverse osmosis system, is very chemically unstable. It is prone to potentially fatal pH drops as acids generated from fish wastes and uneaten food build up. Some buffering is essential, unless the aquarium is constantly monitored.

With acidity, like hardness, the aquarist should work with the fish that are known to prosper in the conditions easily offered. The decision to keep species that cannot do well in the local water supply involves learning more about water chemistry and certainly more work to maintain an aquarium.

Keeping Rare Gouramis

Predictably, most of the lovely but delicate rarities are uncommon in the aquarium world because they have adapted to a narrow niche and cannot adjust to water unlike that in which they have evolved. Specialization can allow a species to colonize a habitat where nothing else can live, but it can also lead to dead ends. One can only speculate about how many beautiful and interesting black-water Anabantoids may have once existed in now-industrialized areas of Southeast Asia. The specialists are always the first to become extinct when environments change. They are also the hardest to keep in aquariums.

Extinction threat: A number of Anabantoids are in danger of extinction, in both Africa and Asia. These tend to be species from limited ranges (South Africa's *Sandelia bainsii*) or animals with very specific environmental needs, like a number of Betta species. The threat to these fish is usually from habitat degradation or introduced, nonnative species. In some cases, the threat comes from other fish commonly kept in aquariums or even other larger Gouramis introduced as food fish. Many Anabantoids start out in habitats that are fragile to begin with. A lot of human interference is not needed to alter their environments fatally.

An extreme habitat: An example of one of these extreme natural Gourami habitats is a natural peat swamp in the Malaysian province of Sarawak, on the western shore of Borneo. One of the authors (O.L.) visited this beautiful habitat in early 2001. Here, the black water was tea colored but clear, over a bottom of fallen leaves, palm fronds, and wood. The swamp was surrounded by thick primary jungle and was much more of what one expects when thinking about collecting tropical aquarium fish in the wild. The water had no measurable mineral content, had a very acidic pH of 4.2, and was a warm 90°F (32°C).

At first glance, the clear, dark water seemed uninhabited. All the cover was on the bottom. One could assume that small fish would not hang around the surface inviting birds to eat them. If Anabantoids lived in such a habitat, they would be very different from the ones encountered in less extreme water conditions close to areas of intense human activity. Many smaller Gouramis and their relatives can breathe surface air but do not necessarily need to surface regularly as their gills can supply them with enough oxygen to survive. Some will build bubble nests underwater or on the bottom sides of leaves or wood. Some will even mouth brood. The latter strategy makes a fish into its own mobile nest, as eggs and larvae are incubated in the mouths of adults. This is common behavior in the genus *Betta* but also occurs in several Gouramis. The individual species descriptions later in this book will specify which species mouth brood.

In the black-water pond at Sarawak, dragging a net through the thick leaf litter on the bottom yielded some treasures. Along with some tiny Rasboras (popular aquarium fish of the Barb group), a number of small Betta species were found. With them were one of the difficult gems of the aquarium world, an underwater nest-building species of Licorice Gourami (in this case probably *Parosphromenus allani*).

Sources of Gouramis

Aquarists always have fun considering how their pets got from their natural habitats to the pet shop. Nearly all Gouramis come from aquarium fish farms of various sizes, mostly around Singapore or in Florida. Small Gouramis of species that would be considered rarities, in commercial terms, are usually caught in the wild. Those who fish these animals want young adults and juveniles, as they survive the rigors of shipping much better than large adult specimens.

All common Asian Gouramis seen in pet stores today are produced in aquaculture ponds on fish farms. For example, *Trichogaster* ponds are 9.8 feet by 9.8 feet (3 m by 3 m) and have a thick *Eichhornia crassipes* as cover for the dense populations of fish. Fry are regularly taken out and transferred to larger growout ponds, which are harvested after six months and sold.

When the fish are ready for export, the jobber takes delivery from smaller farms and breeders (or, with rarities, from those who collected the Gouramis from the wild). The larger fish are stocked in concrete basins, while the dwarf species go into various-sized glass containers until sold. The fish are bagged and sent to the West from Singapore, Malaysia, Thailand, and Indonesia. One relatively small box can contain 500 *Betta splendens* in individual bags or 300 fish the size of a Blue Gourami. Upon arrival at the importer's installation, they are generally put into large display tanks to be bought in small numbers by local pet shops. The details will be discussed later, as they do have a strong bearing on how the aquarist chooses fish for home aquariums.

This manual concentrates on the more adaptable Anabantoids, as they are the ones aquarists have the most questions about. It will, however, introduce the more delicate species for those who catch the Gourami bug and wish to do some exploration. As will be seen, there is a lot more to Gouramis than the dozen or so species that regularly appear in pet stores.

Combtail Gouramis (Belontia sp.) are often found in small ponds.

Blue Gouramis (Trichogaster trichopterus) *can be caught in small streams like this one.*

This white Giant Gourami (Osphronemus gorami) *is enjoying a meal of bloodworms.*

HOW-TO: FEEDING

Most Gouramis are very easy to feed. They will happily accept the commonly available flake and floating pellet foods. If aquarists have access to frozen fish foods, their Gouramis will positively glow. It is that easy. Or is it? Once aquarists leave the beaten track and begin to experiment with keeping the rarer species, they may find things becoming more difficult.

Minor Considerations

There are several minor considerations with feeding the commonly available species. If hobbyists are using dry food, they should have at least three sorts. Aquarists with a small number of fish should buy smaller containers, avoiding the temptation of bulk bargains. These lose too much nutritional value long before they are finished.

Hobbyists should feed their fish sparingly. Overfeeding can kill fish very quickly, as uneaten food will pollute the aquarium's water. Gouramis are prone to packing on weight quickly. Aquarists should give the fish what they will eat in a minute or two and no more. Two small feedings per day are ideal. Overweight fish face some of the

same health challenges as their human counterparts.

Frozen Food

Frozen food has made feeding fish much easier. One block of frozen bloodworms, mosquito larvae, adult brine shrimps, or glassworms can last a very long time in the average aquarist's setup. Hobbyists should never use frozen food that has thawed and been refrozen, as it may be harmful to the fish. These frozen insects or crustaceans are taken readily by even finicky species and seem to improve growth, color, and vitality.

One warning though—many hobbyists, especially those allergic to dust or dust mites, will have reactions to bloodworms. These deep red, midge larvae may be the most popular frozen food, as they are great value for the money, but they are potentially a problem for some. If an aquarist has a skin reaction to the frozen product, he or she should not use the equally convenient freeze-dried bloodworm products, as that person may experience a respiratory reaction.

Live Food

Live food is a necessity for some delicate species and

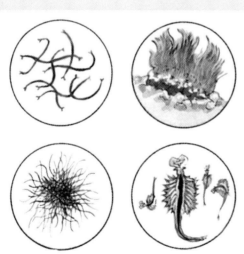

Various types of live food are frequently used to feed Anabantoid fishes. Clockwise from top left: bloodworms, algae, brine shrimp and tubifex worms. Other live foods that are relished include white worms, daphnia, and mosquito larvae.

GOURAMIS

always a welcome treat for others. Many experienced aquarists follow their fish-keeping "bug" into collecting or growing bugs for their pets. Here are some of the live-culture options that are easier to work with.

White worms are small worms, like those sometimes found under rocks in gardens. They can be cultured in huge quantities in plastic margarine or ice cream tubs. They should be kept on damp earth and fed moistened, dry cat food. The small amounts of food should be put under a piece of glass and replaced regularly. The worms do not escape into the aquarist's house, and a well-maintained culture will not smell. A smaller version, the grindal worm, has to be cultivated in very cool conditions.

Cysts or eggs of *Artemia* sp., the brine shrimps, are readily available in aquarium circles. The cysts must be stored cold. For many years, predicting salt-to-water mixes for the popular Utah cysts was easy. The market now offers *Artemia* eggs from China, Russia, many Asian republics, and even Tibet. The hobbyist could begin mixing at a ratio of 1 tablespoon (15 mL) per 1 quart (1 L) of water and go up according to the success one has. Alternatively, he or she could ask at any good pet shop or distributor. These individuals should know the needs of the creatures they are selling. The cyst/eggs need aeration and light, and they can be strained through easily acquired brine shrimp nets. They are wonderful food for both small Gouramis and Bettas and for fry large enough to handle them. Some stores will sell short-lived adults in small bags.

Daphnia are free-swimming crustaceans that most small-to-medium size Anabantoids adore. They can be collected from clean ponds, usually in spring. They are easy to culture outdoors in an old aquarium or tub, shaded and screened on top to keep mosquitoes out. Gouramis will

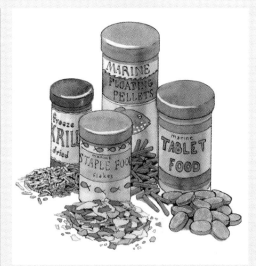

There is a wide variety of dry prepared foods available for the aquarium hobbyist. Not every formulation is right for Anabantoids and the hobbyist should be prepared to do some research. Whatever is fed, care should be taken to avoid overfeeding, which can be disastrous.

devour mosquito larvae. However, intentionally growing them is apt to cause problems with neighbors and is illegal in many areas. Daphnia cause no such problems and can be fed with yeast or moldy vegetables. They are much harder to culture indoors.

Microworms are tiny creatures to be fed to growing fry. They can be cultured in small plastic containers on wet corn meal with yeast. They do produce a slight odor but are excellent food. Other more exotic options range from wingless fruit flies to black worms, tubifex worms, mealworms, or other small insects. All have their strong and weak points. Aquarists should discuss their pros and cons with the source they acquire them from, be it a large pet shop, an aquarium club, or an Internet laboratory or fish food supplies site.

COMMON DISEASES AND PROBLEMS

Gouramis, like all other fish, do develop various diseases at times. The aquarist must always be on the lookout for these. If a single fish displays the symptoms of disease, the aquarist may have to treat the entire aquarium—or all its inhabitants may die.

Parasitic Infections

Velvet

Velvet (also known as oodinium) is caused by the tiny, single-celled parasite *Piscinoodinium pillulare*. An afflicted fish will have tiny white-to-pale-yellow spots on the skin as if it were covered with a thin film of velvet or powdered sugar. In this, velvet closely resembles another common but dangerous parasite, ich. Sometimes the velvet infestation will be limited to the gills. If that occurs, it will cause the fish to scratch frequently on the bottom or decorations, to swim with clamped fins, or to rock back and forth using only its pectorals. This

The most effective strategy for dealing with illness in an aquarium is prevention. If, however, disease does break out in a tank, there are a number of techniques and treatments that can be used to avert disaster.

parasitic disease is easily spread by nets, plants, or transfer of water. It often strikes in dirty water, when fishes' defenses are already challenged by environmental conditions, and seems to like light. It can often be the cause of mysterious fry die-offs. It is extremely hard to detect on tiny young fish but flourishes in the crowded conditions offered to fry.

Many preparations are available for this common disease at pet stores. The best are copper-based medications. However, these are toxic to fish at a pH under 7.

Copper is also extremely toxic to snails and all other invertebrates, such as ornamental shrimps. Salt can be used, after a water change, at a rate of approximately 1 teaspoon (5 mL) per 5 gallons (20 L) of water. Some aquarists will dim the tank lights. Older literature calls for the use of acriflavine, a once-commonly available yellow-green dye that has since been identified as a potential health danger for humans. The best

spots on the skin, fins, and eyes of the fish. The spots can vary in size but are generally slightly smaller than a grain of sugar. The size differences are the result of ich being caused by a number of related species.

Knowing the life cycle of this pest is the key to attacking it. Ich has a free-swimming stage in which it attaches to fish. At this stage, it can be destroyed. Once it has attached, the parasite produces a protective cyst (the white spot observed on the fish). It feeds on the fluids of the fish while in the safety of its cyst, which soon bursts, releasing huge numbers of unprotected parasites. This stage makes treatment easy if the infestation is diagnosed early.

Treatment: Aquarists must always have enough ich medication on hand to treat their fish. Pet stores sell a large number of brands, and all of them work to varying degrees. Persons may have to experiment to find the one that works best in their aquarium conditions. Aquarists must be very cautious about using preparations that contain formalin, formaldehyde, or the very effective medicinal dye malachite green, as these are known carcinogens. If they must be used, avoid contact with skin and wear gloves.

Some preparations have another dye, methelyne blue. This is harmless, although it will color fingers in interesting ways. Many a tank of fish belonging to an unprepared aquarist has been saved by a run to the pharmacy, where methelyne blue is often sold on its own as an ingredient in a home remedy mouthwash recipe.

bet is to consult (quickly) with a local aquarium store and always to keep a supply of medication on hand. This parasite can be hard to eradicate and is very opportunistic. In many cases, it simply survives and waits until the next time your aquarium water becomes polluted. Velvet is common with the small red blackwater *Betta* species and some small Gouramis (Licorice, Croaking, Chocolate, and Colisa).

White Spot

Ich (or ick or white spot) is the number-one killer parasite of aquarium fish. Ich is named for the parasite that causes it—*Ichtyophthirius*. It will find its way into an aquarium at least once (and probably more often than that) in an aquarist's fish-keeping experience. This small protozoan parasite will show up as white

By increasing the aquarium temperature to 85°F (30°C), the bursting of the cyst can be accelerated, allowing treatments to attack the free-swimming protozoans. A light addition of salt can stimulate the fish to develop a thicker protective slime coating, helping them to repel the parasites during this time. After a week, do a water change, siphoning from the bottom. If the ich returns, review aquarium maintenance procedures. Beware of quick temperature drops, as they produce conditions these protozoans love. All small Gouramis, Ctenops, Malpulutta, and some of the Bettas are extremely sensitive to ich. Closely watching the fish is necessary to diagnose infections early.

Bacterial Diseases

Bacterial diseases can break out quickly if the water conditions are less than ideal. Poor conditions can be the result of a clogged filter, poor water-changing regimens, or keeping fish in chemically inappropriate conditions. These killers often come in with newly purchased, unquarantined fish. Keeping a small, fully equipped tank running for new arrivals is always best. However, very few people have the self-discipline not to fill such a tank with permanent residents.

Symptoms of bacterial disease include red sores on the fins, body, or eyes of the fish; protruding eyes; or dropsy—a condition in which the fish bloats and the scales stand away from the body. Dropsy is usually a terminal symptom of an advanced infection of the internal organs of the fish. It is not a disease in itself, although it was often treated as such in older literature. Bacterial infections can sometimes be treated, although treatment remains guesswork for most.

Over-the-counter fish antibiotics and antibacterial drugs are becoming increasingly difficult to find in many jurisdictions. Some, such as tetracycline, have become ineffective because most aquatic pathogens are now resistant. Many Asian keepers have used the leaves of the sea almond tree, or magic almond tree, as an herbal antibacterial in black-water tanks containing Anabantoid species for a number of years now. These leaves, as well as products made from similar natural sources, are coming on to the Western market now, mainly as a nonantibiotic medication. Aquarists should check with local stores to see what treatments are both available and recommended.

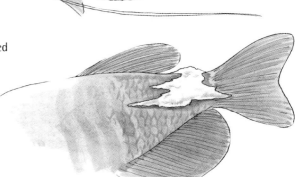

top: Bacterial disease.
bottom: Fungus.

The successful aquarium is a reflection of the fish keeper's knowledge of the fishes in his or her care and the ability to provide species-appropriate living conditions in a controlled environment.

A male Yellow Gourami (Trichogaster trichopterus).

In their normal habitats, many Gourami species can be caught in the drainage ditches usually found at the roadsides.

Collecting Blue Gouramis (**Trichogaster trichopterus**).

Fungi

Fungi (*Saprolegnia* and others) are in every aquarium. However, they are really a secondary symptom that affects fish that have external injuries or are weakened by other diseases. Fish keepers must make sure that the aquarium contains clean water and no damaged fish. This minor (if treated quickly) problem is common among territorial Gouramis and Bettas. Fungi can appear as tufts, fine hairs, or slime on the fins, eyes, or body of infected fish. Often, removing the source of the injuries can stop the disease from spreading further, as the immune system of the fish will then be able to handle the problem itself. The aquarist can physically remove the fungus tufts from the fish and then place the animal into a different aquarium with clean water. A salt bath can help to control the problem. The aquarist should place 0.5 ounces (15 g) of noniodized kitchen salt (rock salt or kosher salt) into 1 quart (1 L) of water and bathe the affected fish for 10 minutes, removing it if it seems to be in distress.

Mycobacteria

Unfortunately fish tuberculosis (TB) is becoming more common. It can be found in both wild-caught and captive-raised fish. It is caused by mycobacteria. This disease is a multi-faceted problem. Gouramis are among the many fish groups more commonly affected by this disease, for which there is no cure. The symptoms resemble those listed under bacterial diseases, including open sores or swelling on the body, deformities, swollen abdomens or foreheads, or scales sticking out. If an aquarist encounters this dangerous illness, ensure that new fish do not have visible signs of the disease, and immediately euthanize any infected fish. Fish TB can infect wounds and open sores on humans, where it can cause painful ridged knots or small sores. The disease is known to doctors as fish tank or swimming pool granuloma. Infections in healthy people is still uncommon. However, older, immunodeficient people or people with open cuts should wear gloves to handle fish or things around the aquarium, especially if this disease has been present. People rarely contract this illness, but caution is always the best policy.

Poisoning

A number of household products can poison fish. Sprays, air fresheners, soap (which strips the slime/immune system from fish), and ammonia-based window cleaners can be deadly. So too are insecticides used in the household. Quick action with massive water changes can be effective. A less easily identified problem is poisoning from municipal water treatment, as systems will sometimes be flushed with high doses of chlorine or chloramine, especially in spring and summer. Aquarists who grow complacent about the use of dechlorinators or chloramine neutralizers to go with their water changes will sometimes be given a sad surprise after a routine water change.

Sterilizing: Just as in human medicine, all tools, tanks, gravel, and so on that have been in contact with sick or dying fish must be sterilized. For this, use common household bleach. Filters, heaters, gravel, and inorganic ornaments can be sterilized by placing them into a covered bucket of water that has 0.5 cup (120 mL) of bleach added. Most aquarists will use a

New additions to an aquarium should be floated in the tank, in the bag they were bought in, for 30 minutes before being freed. This allows the water temperature to equalize.

5-gallon (20-L) food-grade bucket, but one should use equipment that can be handled easily. To clean the tank itself, the same solution can be used. All items that have been in contact with bleach must be rinsed thoroughly and could also be placed outside to dry to evaporate the remaining bleach. Bleach, soap, and antibacterials are very toxic to fish. Even a small amount remaining in the water could kill the fish.

Aquarists should buy one net for each aquarium to avoid the spread of disease from tank to tank. They must never put their hands into the water when feeding fish in several aquariums. They should also wash their hands after doing anything in the tank, as one would after cleaning up after other pets.

For emergencies (fish always become ill on Sunday night), aquarists should keep three basic medications in a fish first-aid kit. Remember, as with any medication, these medications must be kept away from other pets and children—not in the cabinet under the aquarium! Always keep a medication for ich, a copper-based medication for oodinium (this can be used for ich, in a pinch), and if available, a broad-spectrum antibiotic or sulfa drug. These medications are becoming increasingly difficult to find, as their distribution is under stricter controls and may require a prescription from a veterinarian.

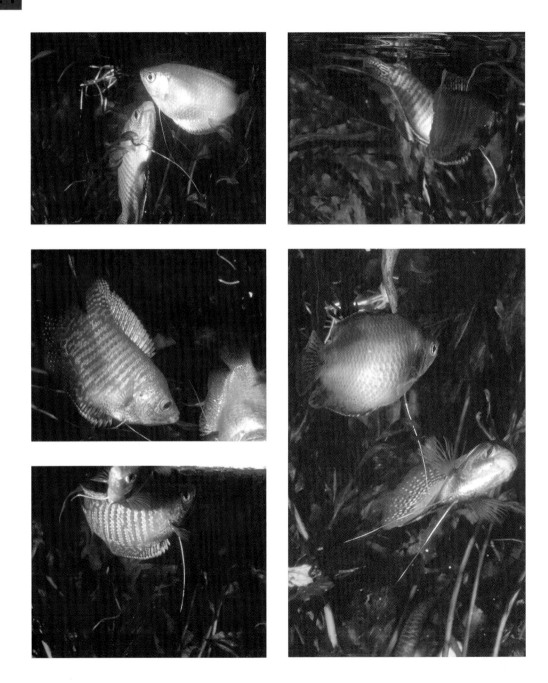

Under the correct conditions, a number of Gourami species will breed readily. In this sequence, a pair of Dwarf Gouramis (Colisa lalia) perform the typical bubble nesters' mating ritual.

Gouramis should be healthy, robust fish. Books on aquarium keeping often advise people to pick up Blue or Lavender Gouramis to cycle their filters, given the fishes' already-noted resistance to bad conditions. This book has already described the conditions under which food-fish Gouramis are commercially farmed in Southeast Asia. With the exception of a few dwarf or black water species, these fish are survivors. So why do so many new Gourami keepers have trouble keeping their fish alive?

Unfortunately, the very hardiness of most popular Gouramis in tanks can work against them in the commercial fish trade. The care fish farms and exporters will take with more delicate animals rarely extends to Gourami shipments. They are raised and transported under crowded conditions, a fact that can lead to their arriving with a wide range of bacterial infections. As well, at any sign of trouble, fish farms will often simply treat them with massive doses of antibiotics. As a short-term strategy, this works. In the long-term, though, it has serious consequences for the health and immune systems of the fish.

The first step in succeeding with Gouramis is to make the right choices. Once aquarists have healthy animals in well-maintained tanks, the chances of their fishes becoming sick are very small.

Choosing a Pet Shop

Aquarists must begin by choosing a pet shop in which they have confidence. They need to look beyond the price tags on the store tanks and try to find a store where the staff show a genuine curiosity about the fish they sell. A good store will choose its fish sources carefully and will not buy from suppliers simply because they offer cheap prices. No reputable aquarium store wants to be known for selling sick fish. Aquarists must look for well-lit, clean aquariums. They should check for dead fish in all the store's tanks to see if attention is being paid to the fish sold. Additionally, if the aquarists can identify any diseases in any of the tanks, they should find out if the sick fish are still for sale. If they are, aquarists should find another store.

Talking to the staff is important. Aquarists should ask a few questions and try to find out when the Gouramis they are considering buying arrived at the store. Giving fish a few days in the display tanks before purchasing them is a good idea. Since most Gourami illnesses are the result of fish farm and shipping conditions, a little patience can save people from some discouraging surprises. Ideally, interested buyers should return to the store at least once before purchasing to see how the fish are doing.

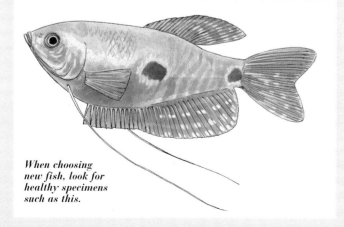

When choosing new fish, look for healthy specimens such as this.

Choosing Gouramis

Aquarists should try to watch the fish being fed to see how they react. Then, they should observe the fins of the fish. Are they held erect? This is a key sign, especially when a lot of potentially scrappy young males are being kept in the same tank. If the fins are spread, interested buyers should look for white spots or white patches of fungus. If the fins are very ragged, beware. This could simply be the result of the fish fighting while crammed together in the bag, but it may also come from a bacterial infection.

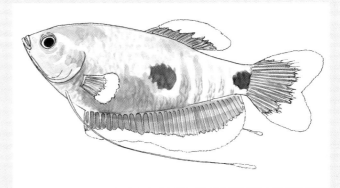

Fin rot, a common disease of aquarium fishes, is caused by poor living conditions.

Interested buyers need to watch how the fish swim. The behavior of Gouramis in pet shops is dull, as the usual bare and overcrowded tanks leave them very little to do. They will certainly not show normal, active behavior in such a stressful environment. However, they should not be lying around on the bottom (a sign of overall poor health) or constantly gasping at the surface. Remember that Gouramis do breathe at the surface. However, after a gulp or two of air, they will generally swim off. A fish that hangs down from the surface may have respiratory problems.

Next, aquarists should look at the weight of the fish. It should be evenly distributed. If the head seems bony or overly large in relation to the flanks, they should avoid buying the fish. Indeed, because of the danger of fish tuberculosis, they should avoid fish from any aquarium in which this symptom occurs.

A look at the scales of the fish comes next. If they appear to be protruding and the fish appears swollen, the animal is suffering from the final stages of a fatal bacterial infection. Such

an infection usually comes from poor conditions, which suggests even the healthy-looking fish in the same aquarium may be incubating an illness.

Next, aquarists need to check the eyes of the fish. Are they clear or milky? Do they seem to be protruding?

Most of the Gouramis seen in a good aquarium store will show none of the symptoms above. If one can avoid bringing home already diseased specimens, then the new Gouramis should settle in nicely.

Illnesses

Assuming aquarists have invested time in prevention, diseases should be an uncommon problem for the fish once they are home. Well-chosen, well-fed Gouramis in clean tanks rarely become ill. However, the introduction of unquarantined new fish or plants, equipment failures, and bad luck are always out there.

Remember that unless aquarists have a fully equipped laboratory somewhere in their homes, diagnosing and treating illnesses will always involve guesswork.

THE GOURAMI AQUARIUM

Every aquarium keeper wants a beautiful tank. To reach this easily accomplished goal, all one needs is a little planning. The trick is to strike a balance between the aquarist's wish to observe lots of colorful, interesting Gouramis and the needs of the fish. This chapter shows how this can be done.

Purchasing the Aquarium

The first rule is to purchase the largest aquarium that space and finances will allow. The larger the aquarium, the more stable it is as an environment. It will offer not only more room to the fish but also more learning space to the hobbyist. Maintaining an aquarium is not a lot of work, but it should be done regularly. In a small tank, fish waste and uneaten food accumulate quickly, polluting the water. If a hobbyist is not prepared to follow a tight maintenance schedule, then the fish will suffer. He or she must always be on top of the maintenance for small tanks. A fish bowl demands ten times the maintenance of a well-set-up 20-gallon (75-L) aquarium. A larger tank still needs to be clean. However, it can be easily set up so it can miss a water change without problems. It will also allow for more plants and, importantly for most hobbyists, more fish.

The water in the natural habitats of the Licorice Gourami is characteristically "tea-colored."

Maintaining the Aquarium

Taking care of a Gourami aquarium is very easy. Just as one must water houseplants, the aquarist must remove and replace water from the fish tank. Ideally, about 25 percent of the water should be changed each week. The filter alone cannot maintain the health of the fish, and pollutants will accumulate in the water.

The simplest method for changing water is to buy a siphon hose and a plastic bucket. This is also the simplest method for taking the fun out of the fish tank. Remember, 1 gallon (4 L) of water weighs about 8 pounds (4 kg). The hobbyist should choose a bucket he or she can comfortably carry when it is full. Lugging large buckets to and from the sink is exercise anyone's back may not want.

If one does take this route, the bucket should not be used for nonaquarium purposes. Fish have a slime covering on their skin, which acts as a first line of defense against pathogens and parasites. Detergent, cleaner, or other chemical residues, even in minute quantities, remove that

Algae

Algae is present in all healthy tanks. Many aquarists find it unsightly, while others could not imagine a tank without it. If it collects on the leaves of slow-growing plants, many types of algae can be simply rubbed off. On the front glass, a scraper can be used, but here one must be careful not to scratch the glass. If colonies of brown algae develop, it indicates low light levels. Black, hairlike algae is a troublesome pest on plants. Infested leaves must be removed. Strong-smelling, slimy, blue-green algae is actually a bacteria known as cyanobacteria. It comes with water pollution but is hard to eradicate. An old trick not often used nowadays is to turn off the aquarium lights and darken the tank for up to a week. Higher plants will survive, but quick-growing algae can be knocked into apparent dormancy. Using algicides are not recommended in closed aquarium systems.

slime and are therefore often fatal to fish. A good option is to buy a water-changing system. Usually, this consists of a hose with a swimming pool type of water-changing device at one end. When attached to a faucet, it pumps out the aquarium using water pressure, and then, with a simple readjustment of the connection, refills it. Initially, it will cost much more than a bucket. However, it is an easy solution when tank maintenance becomes a chore.

Either way, what matters most with aquarium maintenance is consistency. Another good investment (essential with an undergravel filter) is a gravel vacuum. This is a simple plastic tube that attaches to a siphon hose and allows the hobbyist to remove waste from the sand or gravel. While working on the tank, the aquarist can trim or prune the live plants and clean the filter as per the manufacturer's instructions. Remember to unplug the heater before working on the tank and not to plug it back in until all the work is done.

The Stand

Finding a strong, sturdy, and attractive stand is essential. The hobbyist must remember that 1 gallon (4 L) of water weighs approximately 8 pounds (4 kg) and plan accordingly. Most full Gourami tanks will not challenge the strength of typical floors. Over time, though, they can be too much for some tables or bookcases.

A wide variety of aquarium stands are available in any good aquarium store. The hobbyist should make certain the stand chosen is solid; no one would want a tank to wobble. The aquarist must also make certain the stand and tank together are tall enough for that person to be able to observe the Gouramis at the surface.

Traffic patterns: Generally, Gourami watching is best done from the comfort of a chair, which brings up the all-important question of aquarium placement. The tank should be in a quiet place where the hobbyist can be comfortable observing it. It should be in a low-traffic area so that the fish are not constantly spooked by passing people. Remember that fish are very sensitive to vibrations passing through their water, and that jumping children or booming stereos can be quite stressful to them.

A bucket and length of hose are required
for changing the water in an aquarium.

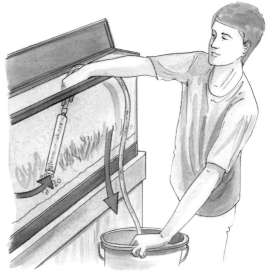

Electricity: Placing the aquarium close to the necessary electrical outlet is important. It is also a good idea to consider carefully where the tank will be in relation to the doors and windows. Gouramis look astonishing in natural sunlight. However, when no one can see the fish because of sunlight-generated algae on the glass, that truth will not give much pleasure. Constantly scraping algae off the glass is a chore to be avoided, as are the scratches on the glass that go with it. Diffused sunlight in a bright room is not going to give the tank problems. However, many aquarists like to keep their tanks in areas where only the lights in the hood illuminate the aquarium.

Drafts: Another consideration specific to Gouramis is cold drafts. Remember, unless one lives in a tropical environment, the aquarium water will have to be electrically heated. Gouramis breathe surface air, which ideally should be very close to the temperature of the water. A tight glass cover will help maintain stability between the two environments. However, it will function less well if the winter air rushes across the tank every time the doors or windows open. Additionally, an aquarium should not be placed too close to a home-heating vent or system. The aquarist should be able to maintain consistency in the environment offered to his or her fishes. The hobbyist should plan ahead to make certain the Gouramis can live in a stable, healthy habitat.

Household products can be problematic for all fish tanks. A kitchen is a bad location for an aquarium due to cooking residues settling onto the surface of the water. Hobbyists should be careful about using household sprays, soaps, cleaners, or chemicals where they can get into the water. One often-overlooked problem can be the use of ammonia-based glass cleaners on aquariums. If these products are used, one must make certain they do not get into the aquarium water. Toxic ammonia, as will be explained in the section on filtration, is a major problem in fish tanks.

Structural integrity: Modern silicone tanks are surprisingly strong, but that strength should not be taken for granted. No one should ever pick up an aquarium with water in it. Even if that person can manage the weight of the water, there is no guarantee the structure of the tank can. Hobbyists should make certain their tanks are placed onto a level surface. Many fish keepers will add insurance by putting Styrofoam sheets or strips of foam-backed carpeting under their tanks to help absorb any unevenness under their aquariums.

Stocking Gourami Tanks

Overstocking the tank is the most common error made by new fish keepers. After all, there are a lot of Gourami species, and they are all intriguing. Add the possibility of other fish in a community aquarium setting, and the temptation to add just one (or ten) more fish can be overwhelming. Overcrowding has serious consequences in a closed aquatic system.

Fish wastes: To begin, levels of fish waste versus water easily get out of control. Even hardy air breathers like Gouramis will be stressed by water pollution, especially if the water is also too crowded for them to satisfy their behavioral needs for territory. Stress leads directly to disease, usually preceded by a loss of color and vitality among the fish. If the aquarium is overstocked, the hobbyist will first lose the very things that made the fish attractive in the first place. Then, he or she will probably lose the fish if that person has not already given up because of the amount of work an overstocked aquarium demands. Setting the goal of keeping 1 inch (2.5 cm) of fish per 1 gallon (3.8 L) of water is better. This rule is imprecise, as 1 inch (2.5 cm) of heavy-bodied *Colisa lalia* (the Dwarf Gourami) is a lot more fish than 1 inch (2.5 cm) of a slender-bodied *Trichopis pumila* (the Dwarf Croaking Gourami). The rule favored by the authors is for the aquarist to calculate exactly how many fish he or she thinks the tank can safely hold, then never put nearly that many into it. With that approach, the fish keeper can relax and enjoy a happy aquarium.

Tank shape: With the possible exception of hexagonal tanks (which have a small water surface and are therefore inappropriate for Gouramis), the shape of the tank is not important. A look at a Gourami's warm, shallow environment might make someone inclined to keep these fish in shallow, low aquariums. This will work perfectly well for the fish. However, in any tank, most Gouramis will be found close to the surface anyway. A low tank placed so that only a contortionist can see the surface is not going to hold someone's interest for long. Tall tanks with only Gouramis in them may appear empty to the casual observer, although this can be easily solved if the fish keeper builds a community of compatible fish around the Gouramis.

In choosing companions, several routes can be taken. One is to stock with fish and plants from the region in which the Gouramis originated. This takes some research but produces a satisfying nature-type tank. The hobbyist can also use an international community tank, with *Corydoras* or Tetras from South America, Loaches from Asia, Killifish from Africa, and Gouramis from both Asia and Africa. The possibilities are limited by only the environmental needs of the fishes, the compatibility of the behavior of the fishes, and the local availability of different species. There are some tried-and-true rules of thumb to follow. One should never put a fish he or she has not read about into a community tank. The hobbyist should keep species with the same territorial needs together, or one will be beaten. Finally, the fish keeper must not put overly active species in with slow-moving, placid Gourami species.

Filtration

How water quality is maintained will have a lot to do with determining if the aquarium is successful. The use of a filter, versus the old technique of doing several water changes weekly in an unfiltered tank, is highly recommended.

However, not all of the systems on the market can be recommended for Gouramis.

Biological filters make use of bacteria to minimize the negative effects of decay (of plants, excrement, uneaten food, and dead fish) on the closed system. All of these factors will produce ammonia (NH_3) or nitrate (NO_3) as a by-product. Another source of ammonia is the exhalation of the fish. Ammonia is toxic to fish, with the toxicity increasing as the pH get higher (more alkaline). A biological filter favors the growth of bacteria that consume ammonia, converting it into less toxic nitrite (NO_2). Other bacteria in the filter convert nitrite to even less dangerous nitrate. Nitrate levels are reduced during the regular 25 percent water changes. Most conventional filters lack the surface capacity to allow for the measurable reduction of nitrate by bacterial action. Such bacteria usually require anoxic (no oxygen) conditions. However, some bioengineered strains are coming onto the market that should perform this function in a normal filter.

To understand the processes in a biological filter, one has to step back and change his or her view of a filter as a machine. These filters are better seen as habitats for desirable bacterial life. Just as the filter helps keep fish alive, the aquarist has to do some things to get the filter going too. This book has described how Gourami species like *Trichogaster trichogaster* (the Blue Gourami) come from less-than-pristine water conditions. They can often tolerate life with a new biological filter. A biological filter can take four to six weeks to be adequately colonized by beneficial bacteria. During this time, the water quality will not be good. It is important to stock very lightly for the first six weeks and then gradually add fish to a reasonable population level. Some fish are needed at the start to "feed"

the filter. If too many are used, the new system will crash. The water test kits sold in aquarium stores can be useful for monitoring these early stages in the life of a biological filter.

Starter colonies of beneficial bacteria can be purchased in good pet shops or online. If added to the water after dechlorination, they can jump-start a biological filter. Gravel from an established tank can also be used, although it does not work as quickly as a starter culture. However, building up the population of a tank slowly is still advisable to allow the system to stabilize.

High-powered filters can offer excellent biological filtration, but so can old-fashioned, air-driven sponge filters. Lower-turnover filters can be good for bubble-nesting Gouramis, as they do not create much of a nest-destroying current at the surface.

Mechanical filters are limited in their use. They make the water look good but do not necessarily improve its quality. Their job is to remove solid sediments from water. They are best used along with biological filters.

Commercial chemical filters usually use charcoal or resins to remove elements from water. They are best used in conjunction with biological systems. One type of chemical filtration that appeals to many Gourami keepers is peat filtration. It can be messy and is usually homemade, but it can be very useful. Either aquarium-grade or very coarse insecticide/fertilizer-free garden peat moss is thoroughly soaked or even boiled. (Do not boil it in an aluminum pot.) It is then added to a nylon bag in the filtration system. The peat moss will remove water-hardening minerals from the water while releasing acidic tannins into the aquarium. This will have three main effects.

First, it acidifies the water, dropping the pH. Second, tannins seem to contain chemicals that can stimulate reproductive activity in rain forest fish. Finally, it stains the water. Water colored light brown to sepia does not appeal to all, but it does do remarkable things to the already beautiful colors of fish like Honey Gouramis *(Colisa chuna),* the *Trichopsis* species, and the Licorice Gourami group. For the latter group of aquarium rarities, using peat filtration is close to essential.

Filters on the Market

A good aquarium retailer will have a variety of filtration options available. In many cases, the availability of products will change from region to region. Therefore, a hobbyist should consult with knowledgeable employees in a trusted store to see what options are suggested.

Outside power filters pull water from the tank into a box outside the tank, run it through a biological filter (usually a sponge or a type of pleated absorbent material), and,

TIP

Safety Issues

The aquarist must make certain all electrical appliances used for aquariums are secured from falling into the water. Those that do come into contact with the water should be approved by the standards association of the hobbyist's country. All electrical appliances should be disconnected before the Gourami keeper puts his or her hands into the water.

optionally, run it through a chemical medium. The sponge or other biological medium doubles as a mechanical filter, a drawback as they can become clogged. A variation is the popular cannister filter. It draws the water into a sealed cannister for mechanical, chemical, and biological filtration. These are efficient but can be annoying to keep clean. Since they are sealed, monitoring their cleanliness can also be hard. Many outside filters pour the water back with great force. This circulates heat and oxygen in the tank. However, it may agitate the surface too much for bubble nest–building Gouramis. The current generated can be a drawback for still-water fish. If the aquarist keeps Gouramis with no plans to breed them (or keep the less common mouthbrooders), an outflow offering a few still places for the fish to rest is enough. High-outflow filters will wreak havoc on many smaller floating and unrooted plants, clogging their own intakes in the process.

Undergravel filters, powered by either air pumps or powerhead underwater pumps, are an older technology. They draw water through the tank bed, ideally made of about 2 inches (5 cm) of gravel. The bacteria in the gravel perform excellent biological filtration. However, the gravel bed can become clogged with debris and rapidly lose its efficiency. When used with regular gravel vacuuming and water changes, live plants, and light stocking, they are excellent filters for Gouramis. They do not work well if the tank is overly crowded.

Air pump–powered filters: Sponge and box filters are both fine for smaller Gourami tanks. The first provides biological filtration by drawing water through a bacteria-loaded sponge. It does clog with time. Running two in a tank is best. This means that when one sponge is being cleaned (which often temporarily drops the bacterial population), the fish will not be unprotected. Plastic box filters are designed as air-driven mechanical filters. However, they can be modified with sponge inserts or a layer of small lava rocks or gravel on the bottom as a home for bacteria.

Advanced systems: Trickle filters are large and expensive, but they are very efficient for biological filtration. They are not often used for Gouramis unless as part of a central system with many aquariums on one filter. Fluidized bed filters are a recent innovation but are not really necessary for Gourami keeping.

Heating Tanks

Most Gourami species like their environment warm. A good heater becomes necessary. While a quality submersible heater will cost more than a clip-on heater that hangs on the back, it will be much more efficient for Gourami tanks. With clip-ons, the water must be kept close to the highest possible level for safe functioning. Submersibles allow the fish keeper to leave a couple of inches at the top of the tank. This allows one to observe bubble nests, keep the floating plants beloved by Gouramis, and maintain a good area of warm humid air for the fish to breathe. They also allow for a tighter aquarium cover. Under average circumstances, the general recommendation is for 3 to 5 watts of heater strength per 1 gallon (4 L) of water.

A trustworthy thermometer is another necessity, as heaters do sometimes malfunction. Monitoring the temperature daily can save a precious aquarium from becoming a soup bowl. Unfortunately, the temperatures of tanks with less expensive, lower-quality heaters must be checked at least twice daily, as jammed thermostats are a consistent cause of fish death.

Lighting

Lighting is almost a book in itself. Keeping planted aquariums is an engrossing hobby that can easily be combined with Gourami keeping. Generally, fluorescent lighting is recommended for Gourami tanks, with different intensities dependent on tank size and plant choice. Most Gouramis look their best under uneven lighting, with areas of shade provided by floating plants. Under too strong lighting, their often delicate colors will wash out. A great investment is a simple light timer. By being able to regulate the time of the lighting even when not present, the Gourami keeper will be able both to provide a more stable environment and to grow plants.

Plants

Gouramis look great in planted tanks. However, an underwater green thumb can take time and effort to develop. Choosing plants as carefully as one chooses fish can go a long way. With one of the many aquatic plant fertilizers on the market and adequate lighting, the rudiments of this aspect of aquarium keeping should be easy to master.

Finding quality plants can be the same sort of quest as the search for healthy fish. Not all the species listed here will be available in every market, although the expansion of the Internet and mail-order companies is making tracking down rarities increasingly easier. The aquarist is always better off buying plants he or she has seen. This brings the hobbyist back to the need to find a good local shop.

The types of plants chosen depends very much on the type of Gouramis one enjoys. Climbing Perch *(Anabas)*, Giant Gouramis *(Osphronemus)*, and Kissing Gouramis *(Helostoma)* are like lawn mowers in a fish tank. *Trichogaster* and *Colisa* species need floating plants and show very little interest in the bottom. Croaking Gouramis *(Trichopsis)* like broad-leaved substrate plants to build their nests under. The Licorice Gouramis *(Parosphromenus)* group need the same but also call for acid-tolerant choices. Luckily, there are easy-to-keep plants for all of these setups.

Tall-Substrate Plants

Several aspects must be studied before choosing substrate plants. The hobbyist must consider how tall the plant grows (determining where in the tank it will be planted), what water conditions are needed, and, most importantly, the light requirements of the species. Gourami tanks need floating plants, which makes plants needing intense lighting much less interesting.

***Myriophyllum** is a fast-growing plant affording cover to many fish species.*

Vallisneria americana (var. gigantea) is a tall, grasslike plant that needs moderate light. It is ideal for the deep tank. Its wide, grassy leaves will trail over the surface and look especially good in a tank with a current.

Vallisneria tortifolia is a smaller, aquatic grass that will spread quickly in moderate light and can survive well in dim light. It is excellent at the back of a standard-size aquarium. Its spread may have to be controlled, as it will rapidly fill in many of the areas created as open swimming spaces for bottom-oriented species.

Sagittaria subulata is a grassy plant that likes medium light. There is a related dwarf species, *S. pusilla*, that grows to 4 inches (10 cm) and will spread along the foreground. *S. subulata* will reach 24 inches (60 cm).

Bacopa spp. *(caroliniana or monnieri)* are good for a well-lit tank with a space between the cover and the water. These stalky, round-leaved, North American plants will produce small but elegant flowers at the water surface. They have a tendency to lose the leaves at their base as they grow taller.

Cabomba caroliniana is a lovely plant commonly available from outdoor cuttings, but it does poorly in most fish tanks. It needs intense light. It is a great seller in stores. However, few aquarists succeed in keeping it for long.

Myriophyllum spp.: Several species of *Myriophyllum* are available. However, this aquatic pest is illegal to own in some regions. It has spread far beyond its native range and is a serious aquatic invader plant in many regions. For all its beauty, it is a marginal Gourami plant at best due to its need for intense light.

Hygrophilia difformis is an excellent candidate. It can be grown floating or rooted. It does not like mineral-poor water and will either grow rapidly or not at all. If an aquarist is successful with this usually easy plant, the tank will be overrun without regular removal of excess plants.

Hygrophilia polysperma roots and grows quickly under moderate light. It needs trimming, otherwise it will take on a decidedly palm tree–like shape, losing its leaves closer to the bottom. The related *H. corymbosa* is a little more difficult, especially in its light-loving red forms.

Ludwigia repens is a hardy, attractive plant with a need for bright light.

Rotala spp. *(macrandra or rotundifolia)* are generally available as cuttings. If they take hold in a tank, they are lovely plants. However, they do best under moderately bright light.

Medium-Height Substrate Plants

These plants will rarely get to the surface in the average tank. Therefore, they are excellent as foreground vegetation.

Cryptocoryne spp., or crypts, as they are commonly called, are almost a hobby in themselves. A bewildering number of different plants are in this genus. In pet shops, they are often misidentified. In most aquarium books, their complexity is glossed over. Unless a Gourami keeper is in contact with an aquatic plant specialist or nursery, which type of crypt that individual has may always remain a mystery. This is no problem, as these are superb substrate plants for the Anabantoid tank.

Crypts will grow well under the types of conditions favored by most small Labyrinth Fish species. They prosper in soft and acidic water.

They grow slowly and steadily under fairly dim light. They will also flourish under medium lighting, spreading rapidly along the bottom of the tank via runners.

The main practical differences between species is size. Some will reach 20 inches (50 cm) or more, while others stay very small at 4 inches (10 cm). Consulting with a plant dealer or checking a quality plant book prior to buying is best.

Crypts are excellent in tanks for submerged, bubble-nesting Gouramis. The sight of the tiny *Trichopsis pumila* guarding a bubble nest on the reddish underside of a healthy *Cryptocoryne* is not one an aquarist quickly forgets.

Echinodorus spp. (Amazon swords) come in a bewildering range of species and sizes. Most need medium-to-bright light and do best with fertilization. The most attractive versions are centerpiece plants for the decorated aquarium. When happy, they spread quickly.

Hydrocotyle leucocephala (water pennywort) produces round, lily pad–like leaves that can provide good cover to surface-spawning Gouramis. They need light, but this is less of a problem as the leaves grow to the surface. This plant will also try to leave the tank and can spread right across the tank hood if left to run. Specimens on top of the tank cover make for an unexpected display, but the submerged sections lose their lovely leaves.

Aponogeton spp. are bulb plants with varying periods of dormancy. *Aponogeton crispus* are the best option for most aquariums.

Ceratopteris thalictroides (water sprite) is a commonly available, easily grown medium-light plant. It is an excellent organic filter for toxic substances in the fish tank.

Nymphaea spp. are bulb plants and excellent candidates for medium-light tanks. The surface

Planting Technique

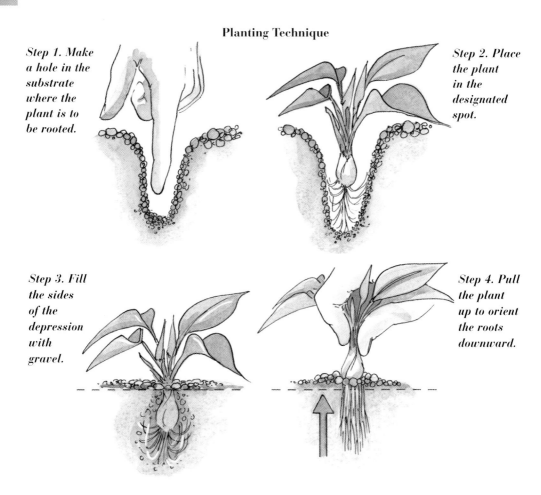

Step 1. Make a hole in the substrate where the plant is to be rooted.

Step 2. Place the plant in the designated spot.

Step 3. Fill the sides of the depression with gravel.

Step 4. Pull the plant up to orient the roots downward.

leaves feed the growth of the bulb but may overly shade the tank. Trimming is a necessity.

Epiphytic (Rhizome-Rooted) Plants

These low-light, easy-to-grow plants are highly recommended for Gourami tanks. They produce root structures that cannot be buried, but rather should be tied onto rocks or driftwood. Buried rhizomes rot, but tied-on structures will attach to their hosts.

Bolbitis heudelotti is an attractive African fern that spreads well under low-to-moderate light with a slight water current. It can be hard to find but is worth the effort. It grows slowly and may need to be cleaned. Its tough leaves grow and spread slowly but steadily.

Anubias spp.: There are a number of attractive *Anubias* species. These slow-growers do well under dim light and will grow steadily under brighter conditions. *Anubias barteri* variety nana, the Dwarf *Anubias,* is the most common form in aquariums.

Microsorum pteropus (java fern) is a beautiful, incredibly easy-to-keep plant. If tied to a proper substrate under moderate lighting, it will spread steadily. Its long, elegant leaves provide an excellent backdrop to colorful Gourami species. The hobbyist should not despair if this pricey plant disappears. *Microsorum* have been known to reappear in tanks months after they seemed to have died.

Vesicularia dubyana (java moss) can be attached to driftwood or rocks. It is an attractive, dim-light plant that can be used to decorate an Anabantoid tank and is rich in fry-feeding microorganisms. Beware, it will choke the intakes of power filters.

Floating, Rootless Plants

Floating plants are extremely useful for all Gouramis. They provide calming cover for bottom-oriented species and also nesting areas and materials for surface bubble nesters. Due to their structures, they also draw nutrition from the aquarium's water—a process quite helpful for maintaining good conditions. Their leaves are also host to a wide range of microscopic food favored by Anabantoid fry.

Ceratophyllum demersum (hornwort) will grow rapidly under good surface lighting. However, if unhappy, it will dissolve and pollute a tank just as quickly. Once established, it is an excellent, hardy candidate for Gourami tanks.

An attractive, well-planted aquarium.

For many newcomers to the hobby, it seems to be the only plant that will grow. Once it survives acclimation to a tank, it is a quick and easy grower.

Riccia fluitans can be a touchy plant to grow. It needs bright light but will grow in mats that shade the tank and hide (and nourish) fry. Once established, it is an excellent nest-building material. It likes soft water.

Plastic Plants

Although purists might disagree, plastic plants can also have their place in the Gourami aquarium. However, they are not useful to those species that incorporate pieces of vegetation into the floating nests. Obviously, they have no biological or filtering function.

A word of warning to hobbyists contemplating keeping *Osphromenus* spp. Giant Gouramis. These voracious vegetarians cannot be kept with any plant. Indeed, once plastic plants develop apparently tasty algae colonies on their leaves, even they will be eaten.

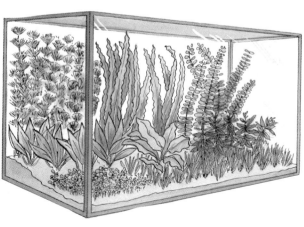

Gourami Behavior

Gourami behavior and aquarium plants are logically linked, as fish behavior is deeply connected to the environment. The gray fish that hover listlessly in a bare, brightly lit pet store tank can become vivid and dynamic animals in an appropriate aquarium habitat. Everything enjoyed about a fish is a product of environment. For fish, even showing color is a social activity.

Color is just one of the ways fish communicate, but it is a key one for hobbyists. In most Labyrinth Fishes, the male displays the colors, either to other males or to females. This is especially true of species that build hard-to-defend floating bubble nests at the surface, like *Colisa lalia, C. chuna,* or *Betta splendens.*

Cryptocorynes are native to many natural Gourami habitats.

Although no observation is 100 percent applicable with Anabantoids, these are also the species with the greatest sexual dimorphism (visible differences between the sexes). Although *Betta splendens* follows its own highly inbred rules, the Gouramis in question will communicate through color intensity. Among Honey Gouramis, the dominant male in a small tank will glow. Subordinate and stressed males, however, will often take on variations on female coloration, to the point where they can be hard to sex in pet stores. In contrast, many male Honey Gouramis kept together in a planted, large aquarium can all

Pistiia *is an ideal plant for covering the surface of the aquarium.*

radiate color if they have enough room to stake out territories worth defending.

It is worth noting that in spite of the obvious courtship behavior of males, female Gouramis are also extremely interesting to watch during courtship. They are very active in making their choices.

Even the hidden bubble nesters (*Trichopsis* and *Parosphromenus,* for example) have environmentally determined coloration. The browns and blacks of the Licorice group are simple camouflage in their dark peat swamp habitats, however striking they are in aquarium tanks.

In bright light, they will fade, as will all the accompanying blues and reds that make the fish so attractive. If these fish feel safe from predators in a darkened tank, they will then turn on their wide range of behavior, including color display.

Hiding places are essential to the beauty of most Gouramis. One of the odd laws of fish keeping is that fish will not usually hide if hiding places are available, but will huddle behind a filter in the absence of hiding places. With many species, providing cover is necessary if the hobbyist is to see the fish. Caves and crevices are also necessary for the health of females in small tanks, should males become aggressive.

Gouramis have evolved several different breeding strategies. Some species lay their eggs and move on with no care for the young. Other species build nests out of bubbles on the surface (some species' eggs float; other species' eggs sink), other species produce hidden, submerged bubblenests, and still others are themselves nests, carrying their eggs and larvae in their mouths. Predictably, there is no one strategy for breeding Gouramis.

Egg Scatterers

The best-known Asian egg scatterer is the Kissing Gourami. Both eggs and larvae have oil globules, allowing them to float on the surface. The parent fish spawn and pay no further attention to the results. The aquarist can either remove all the adult fish in the tank, or collect the eggs for incubation.

Surface Bubble Nesters

Surface bubble nesters produce a foamy air-, saliva-, and sometimes plant-based floating nest at the surface. Betta and *Pseudosphromenus* species produce sinking eggs, while Gourami (*Colisa, Trichogaster,* and *Macropodus*) eggs float. The nest is guarded until the fry are free-swimming. Usually, it is best to spawn these fish in special tanks, set up as smaller versions of the recommended maintenance tank. Removing the parent fish is always easier than trying to catch the tiny, delicate fry.

Hidden Bubble Nesters

Hidden bubble nesters can meet their oxygen needs through the use of their gills, and can therefore stay almost permanently submerged. Their bubble nests are constructed under overhanging leaves or on the roofs of caves. They tend to be small and shy. Examples are the Croaking and Licorice Gouramis.

Dwarf Gouramis spawning.

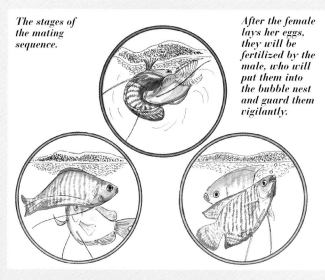

The stages of the mating sequence.

After the female lays her eggs, they will be fertilized by the male, who will put them into the bubble nest and guard them vigilantly.

GOURAMIS

Mouthbrooders

Many hobbyists don't realize many Anaban-toids mouthbrood. These Gouramis and Bettas tend to come from moving water that would destroy bubble nests. They are difficult to breed, as the male (who cares for the eggs and larvae) tends to swallow his charges when stressed. These species can be bred in lightly and carefully stocked community setups. It is unwise to remove the male, as this often provokes an immediate swallowing of the eggs or larvae. A good strategy is to remove all other fish and watch closely for fry. You will not find many, as, compared to often-elaborate bubble nests, mouths hold very few eggs. Many Bettas, plus the Chocolate Gourami group, are the best known of the mouthbrooding species.

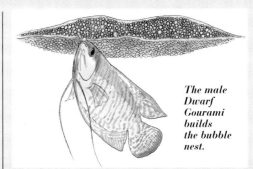

The male Dwarf Gourami builds the bubble nest.

Feeding

Many Anabantoid fry are too small to eat the standard fare for newborns in the fish hobby, freshly hatched brine shrimp. They must be supplied with microorganisms. The inability of hobby-ists to provide adequate quantities of food is the single greatest killer of Gourami and Betta fry.

Solutions involve some work. Starter cultures for microorganisms can be purchased online. Older aquarium sources have a variety of recipes based on turnips, boiled grass, and other vegetable matter combined with pond water that are just as useful, but more work. If you are near an aquarium club, you can learn what is available locally. Otherwise, try the Internet.

As a spin-off from the aquaculture industry, there are now some very small powdered foods. Combined with water and shaken vigorously, they provide a good start.

Spawning

Popular Gouramis like *Trichogaster*, *Colisa*, and *Macropodus* often will readily spawn in community tanks; the challenge for the aquarist is raising the fry. Convincing the more difficult species to breed becomes an interesting challenge to many fish keepers. Here are some ideas you may want to play with.

Fish can become distracted or stressed in an aquarium. Crowding, noisy, and vibrating equipment, aggressive tank mates, and other stresses will sometimes drive fish into "displaced behavior," and possibly cause misdirected energy.

Many of the tiny hidden bubble nesters can't cope with other fish of even their own species in close proximity at breeding time. Try isolating a pair and see what happens. Turn off the lights, leave them in peace, and hope.

Water conditions can be modified in a small breeding tank by adding clean rainwater or reverse osmosis water. Peat filtration can release stimulating tannins, as well as soften and darken water for blackwater species. In regions with iron-poor water, a dose of aquatic plant fertilizer sometimes jump-starts reproductive behavior.

Many fish spawn at the onset of the rainy season. Aquarists will carefully slow down water changes, then suddenly do a large change with slightly cooler, softer water to mimic natural conditions.

Most fish breeding secrets are simply the result of becoming informed and willing to experiment. Luckily, fish breeding experiments are usually fun.

SPECIES DESCRIPTIONS

*Gouramis, as a group, are as diverse
as they are fascinating. The fish
keeper can decide from among
many different species and
varieties. This final chapter
will describe the various types
of Gouramis and Labyrinth Fishes.*

Colisa

If the only Gouramis in this hobby were the
two popular species of *Colisa*, the group would
still have made a significant contribution to
the aquarium world. These small, deep-bodied
Gouramis are popular for all the right reasons—
they are vividly colored, peaceful, fairly easy to
keep, and easy to breed.

What makes them so well suited to aquarium life is their simple environmental needs.
These surface-breathing bubble nesters are
creatures of still water. They come from the
floodplains, irrigation systems, and even rice
paddies from the Brahmaputra River, the
Ganges Delta, Bangladesh, and all the way
into Myanmar. They need clean water but
are very adaptable about water hardness
and pH.

*Their distinctive shapes, brilliant colors,
and adaptability to life in a community
tank distinguish many Anabantoid genera.
Their obvious similarities and striking
differences provide endless fascination
for the aquarium enthusiast.*

Colisa lalia

(Hamilton 1822)

The Dwarf Gourami are small fish. They occur
in the wild with their cousins *C. chuna* and
C. fasciata in the wide delta of the Brahmaputra and Ganges Rivers in Bangladesh and into
Borneo. They grow to a maximum size of
2 inches (5 cm). For their length, they have
stocky, heavy, high-backed bodies.

The fact they come from ponds, irrigation systems, and slow-moving streams in a heavily pop-
ulated and farmed region does not mean they
are tolerant of pollution. However, their labyrinth
organ allows them to survive in low-oxygen situ-
ations. In the aquarium, they like warm water—
high 70s°F (mid-20s°C). The water must be clean.
Otherwise, they are prone to bacterial or parasitic infections. They will prosper in most water
as long as it is not extremely hard or alkaline.
They do best in planted tanks, especially with
floating plants. Tank mates should be peaceful,
as these fish hide when stressed. They are easily
bullied or startled by fast-moving tank mates.

Males are colorful with a sharp point at the
rear tip of the dorsal fin. Females are silvery
with rounded dorsals.

Male *C. lalia* build complicated bubble nests, often incorporating floating plants into the structure. A shallow aquarium, 4 to 6 inches (10 to 15 cm) deep with a submersible heater, a tight cover, and no fish other than the Dwarf Gouramis works best. A male with a nest will then court a female. If she is ready, spawning can take a couple of hours. In typical Gourami fashion, the male will wrap around the female, who will expel several floating eggs. The male collects the eggs, puts them into the nest, and the process begins again. When the female is depleted, the male cares for the nest alone. The female can be removed. Embryos hatch at 12 to 16 hours, although it will take two and one-half to three days for them to be able to swim. The male should then be removed. The keeper should commence feeding with commercial fry food or microorganisms.

In spite of their wide availability in the hobby, these are not always easy fish. Many of the animals sold in pet shops are suffering from poor treatment at the fish farm or in shipping. Healthy *C. lalia* are easy fish to keep but are increasingly hard for hobbyists to find.

So too are natural-looking *C. lalia*. Although the wild form is the most beautiful, a number of selected forms are being produced on fish farms. In some cases, the red predominates (and the blue of the wild fish is lost) or vice versa. The initial interest in these artificially selected forms caused them to be produced in enormous numbers, to the point where the natural-form fish is difficult to locate in some areas. As well, females of the mutant forms seem rare in the shops, a fact that has led to speculation about fish farms using hormones to produce more colorful (and marketable) male fish. Stick to the beautiful wild form, and you will know what you are getting!

Colisa chuna
(Hamilton 1823)

The Honey Gourami is another 2-inch (5-cm) wonder, although it is much lighter bodied than the more popular but stocky *C. lalia*. Its range is narrower, mainly centered around Bangladesh. Males are reddish-brown, deerskin-colored fish with bright yellow dorsals and a deep black mask that runs from the eyes to the base of the anal fin. Females are silvery with a generally light-colored longitudinal stripe.

The first complication with the fish, and the one that has kept it from the popularity it deserves, is its reaction to stress. In a bare aquarium store tank, males can entirely lose their colors, becoming indistinguishable from females. This not only makes choosing pairs difficult but also leaves the uninformed aquarist with the impression of looking at a tank of ugly, plain Gouramis. If a group is bought and put into a peaceful tank with lots of floating plants, healthy males will become absolutely stunning fish within minutes. As long as they are happy, they will maintain their intense and spectacular coloration. In fact, in a tank with small fish, *C. chuna* will rapidly take a dominant role, with vividly marked males parading along the front and even pecking at the glass when their keepers approach. In a large tank, male-only groups will form schools, all carrying full color. Interestingly, in such a situation, when a male leaves the school, he will often leave his colors with it.

They are interesting to breed, using the same techniques as detailed for *C. lalia,* although they seem to handle slightly deeper water better. In a single-species tank, or with small, nonpredatory tank mates in a lightly stocked, heavily planted aquarium, small numbers of babies will grow to adulthood with their parents.

Both mutant and artificially colored versions of *C. chuna* are on the market. However, they are not as dominant in the pet trade as are mutant *C. lalia*. *C. chuna* is a fish that must be sought out. Often, the best way is to order it from a retailer. Many wholesalers keep inexpensive specimens on hand for connoisseurs, but shops will shy away from displaying them due to their gray stress coloration.

Colisa fasciata and Colisa labiosa
(Bloch and Schneider 1801) and (Day 1877)

The Striped Gourami, *C. fasciata,* is from India and Bangladesh. Its length is 4 to 5 inches (10 to 12 cm). The Thick-Lipped Gourami, *C. labiosa,* at 3 inches (6 to 8 cm), is from Myanmar. That much is known. The great question is whether they are distinct species. Many experts feel that these fish illustrate a fundamental problem in the naming of animals. Are they one species with a huge range and differently sized populations at the extreme ends of their geographic spread? Or are they different species? If so, what is the cutoff point between them?

These are not rarities, although their lack of color compared with their cousins makes them much less popular than many other Gouramis. As if to compensate, colored and mutant forms are on the market.

Both these fish are productive spawners. They need larger tanks than the other *Colisa* for the large number of very hungry fry.

Trichogaster

If the hobbyist were to go by the species available in the average small pet shop, he or she could be forgiven for thinking almost all Gouramis were in the small genus *Trichogaster.* These medium-sized, peaceful Gouramis are the most commonly available representatives of the Gourami group. In the general hobby, they are often kept in communities of Tetras, Rasboras, or other small schooling fish. Their role in the design ecology of the community tank is to be a large shape, a placid counterpoint to the constant activity around them. As they cruise through a planted tank, with their ventral fins operating as feelers probing their way forward, they are a lovely sight.

For hardiness and adaptability, they are hard to beat. Chapter 1 described how the authors have seen Blue Gouramis not only in extremely polluted farm ponds but also in fast-flowing, clean streams and flooded forests. The conditions in the average home fish tank are no problem for these superb survivors. As long as the fish keeper respects the basic rules of aquarium water maintenance and gives them room to swim, *Trichogaster* Gouramis can adapt to the conditions offered.

Trichogaster leerii
(Bleeker 1852)

The Pearl Gouramis are a delicately patterned midsized Gourami, 4 to 7 inches (12 to 17.5 cm) long or smaller. They are a very popular and available aquarium fish. Males have reddish chests and longer dorsal and anal fins. However, these characteristics do not show clearly until the fish are close to adult size. Although they are a large-bodied animal, they have both the mouth and the peaceful character of a much smaller fish. It is important to avoid keeping *T. leerii* with aggressive fish or nippy species like the popular Tiger Barbs.

A wild male Dwarf Gourami (Colisa lalia).

A female Dwarf Gourami (Colisa lalia).

The "Neon Red" form of the Dwarf Gourami.

The "Neon Blue" form of the Dwarf Gourami.

They do not defend themselves well against faster fish.

Pearls do best in larger tanks, as befits their size. Planting is important. If the hobbyist wishes to see the full effect of their patterning and coloration, shading is essential. Bright lighting blanches their colors. Filtration that produces a strong current should be avoided. They can be kept at temperatures from the low 70s°F to low 80s°F (21°C to 27°C), although the high range is necessary for breeding.

These fish, which in nature generally occur in the shadows under floating plants or along the shallows beside the overgrown banks of

streams in Malaysia, Borneo, and Sumatra, are bubble nesters. If the aquarist wishes to breed them, they must be kept in pairs in their own tank, with lots of hiding places for the female. The male guards the nest. The fry can be raised starting on paramecia, very small powdered food, or liquid fry food until they are large enough to handle freshly hatched brine shrimp and crushed flake food.

All *Trichogaster* have a reputation for occasional aggression, although the Pearl Gourami might be the most peaceful of the group. This aggression is a problem when territorial males are kept together in tanks that are too small or

Two male Honey Gouramis (Colisa chuna) *in a spar.*

A color-injected Thick-lipped Gourami (Colia labiosa).

The Pearl Gourami (Trichogaster leerii).

The Blue Gourami (Trichogaster trichopterus).

The Lavender Gourami (Trichogaster trichopterus).

The Platinum Gourami (Trichogaster trichopterus).

that lack hiding places. Under these conditions, the dominant male's constant picking at subordinate males can be a disturbing and unpleasant spectacle. Males can also be aggressive to females at breeding time. Generally, these disputes are nowhere nearly as violent as what is found among the popular Cichlid group of aquarium fishes. However, dominated *Trichogaster* with nowhere to escape to can be gradually harassed to death.

Trichogaster trichopterus trichopterus and Trichogaster trichopterus sumatranus

(Pallas 1777) and (Ladiges 1933)

In the days before the introduction of Lake Malawi Cichlids into the aquarium hobby, the Blue Gourami, *T. trichopterus sumatranus,* was THE blue fish. Its popularity has faded somewhat, though its colors have not. When happy, these hardy and interesting Gouramis are very blue, with two dark spots along their flanks. Males have longer, sharper fins than females, who are generally smaller. They grow to 4.5 inches (12 cm) and should be kept in tanks large enough to allow them plenty of swimming room. The less colorful but more widely distributed *Trichogaster trichopterus trichopterus* is a grayish blue fish, often sold as the Lavender Gourami. The trade names on these related fish are not very helpful or descriptive.

In too-small tanks, they can be mildly aggressive, especially if they decide to spawn. Older specimens can sometimes become grouchy. Males are ferocious defenders of their nests!

T. trichopterus trichopterus come from most of southeast Asia and have been introduced into continental Africa, Madagascar, South America, and the Caribbean islands. The *T. trichopterus sumatranus* subspecies comes from the island of Sumatra but may also have been introduced to other habitats. Such unintended introductions of invasive species have been an unfortunate side effect of the growth of the aquarium hobby. Under no circumstances should hobbyists ever release their fish into the wild, as such actions can have serious and unpredictable ecological repercussions. Like all *Trichogaster,* both subspecies can be kept and bred in the setup described for *T. leerii.*

Of special interest is their habit of eating hydra, a tiny, stinging invertebrate predator that is not only unsightly in tanks, but can eat the small fry of many popular species. Breeders using live baby brine shrimp as a first food can often face major hydra infestations. They will sometimes put Blue Gouramis into a future fry-rearing tank to clean it up before using it for the young of the fish they breed. Blue Gouramis also get stuck with the unenviable task of cycling biological filters, as they can survive the poor water conditions offered by a new filter much better than most other species.

Trichogaster trichopterus

The three color variations of *Trichogaster trichopterus*—the Cosby Gourami, the Golden (or Yellow) Gourami, and the Platinum (or Silver) Gourami—may be more available than the original wild forms of the fish. All are the product of selective breeding programs, as naturally occurring mutations in color patterns were line-bred to produce true breeding forms. The Cosby Gourami has lovely dark blue side blotching, especially when it is young. Both the Golden and Silver Gourami varieties display what their names imply. These highly inbred forms are generally smaller and less hardy than the wild forms of the fish. In a way, they are a holdover from an earlier period, when *T. trichopterus* was an extremely popular aquarium fish. Many aquarists worked with these animals prior to their being pushed aside by the explosion of new and exotic species in the latter part of the twentieth century. That many mutant color forms appeared in tanks is a measure of how many tanks these fish once lived in.

Trichogaster pectoralis
(Regan 1909)

Snakeskin Gouramis were also much more popular in the past than they are now. These large Gouramis grow up to 8 inches (20 cm) in length, although they are usually 6 inches (15 cm) long. They lack the vivid colors of their cousins, although they have attractive patterns on their flanks. They are as likely to be found pickled in jars at larger Asian grocery stores as they are to be seen swimming in aquariums. Although they originated in Vietnam, Thailand, and Cambodia, like many food fish, they have been introduced into a number of other regions.

They need a large aquarium to provide swimming room and like a temperature in the high 70s°F (25°C to 28°C). Their bubble nests can produce huge numbers of tiny fry. They are quite peaceful, although they can be expected to defend their nests energetically.

Trichogaster microlepis
(Guenther 1861)

Moonlight Gouramis do not show their translucent coloration well in brightly lit aquarium store tanks. Therefore, like many delicately colored fish, they do not have the popularity they deserve. These fair-sized Gouramis

grow up to 8 inches (20 cm). They are extremely gentle and peaceful creatures.

Adult males have reddish chests with an overall blue-green glow to their bodies. Females are silvery, with a short and less pointed dorsal fin. They are very productive breeders that like to use pieces of plants in their bubble nests. As a measure of their adaptability, these Thai and Cambodian fish are found in habitats ranging from small shallow ponds and sidearms (with *Betta splendens* as neighbors) to the margins of large lakes.

These fish owe much of their luminous beauty to their small scales. This has a downside, as their reduced defenses mean they are quite susceptible to ich parasites.

Helostoma—Kissing Gouramis

Helostoma temminckii
(Cuvier and Valenciennes, 1831)

The Kissing Gourami is an old standard of the aquarium hobby that is thankfully going out of fashion. In reality, this is not a good fish for the average tank, as it is a bruiser that can top out at 1 foot (30 cm) in length. Once the heavy body of the fish and its enormous appetite are factored in, one is left with an animal that will not only be cramped in the average aquarium but will also challenge the efficiency of any filter. It is a great fish for a Gourami specialist with a very large aquarium. So why has this Southeast-Asian food fish been a popular pet, for years, available in most small neighborhood pet shops?

This oddball Gourami originated in Thailand. However, just like most easily pond-farmed

The Cosby Gourami (Trichogaster trichopterus).

The Moonlight Gourami (Trichogaster microlepis).

The Snakeskin Gourami (Trichogaster pectoralis).

A freshly caught Blue Gourami.

food fish, its wild range has long since been extended. It is an algae eater par excellence with thick, protruding lips, each of which features several rows of movable teeth. When combined with the very efficient, plankton-sifting gill structures, these make the one species of *Helostoma* very efficient algae eaters.

The lips also make these fish popular, as they are famous for their "kissing" behavior. These fish will push their toothy lips forward and lock onto the lips of other *Helostoma*. They will then push each other around the tank. To the disappointment of many fish keepers, this activity is not directly connected to courtship. It has, however, caused many juveniles of these large kissing fish to be kept in small tanks.

Most of the time, the fish available in the trade is a pink-to-white color mutant. Recently, a marbled version and a deformed balloon variant have become available. The wild form of the fish is more green to gray, with light brown, horizontal stripes.

The fish is a bit of an anomaly. Although its feeding and anatomic features are highly specialized, its breeding strategies and ecological needs are not. It can do well in almost any freshwater conditions at temperatures in the high 70s°F (25°C). In the wild, they breed at the start of the rainy season. An adult female can produce up to 10,000 floating eggs. These are not only not cared for but actively eaten by the parents. In aquariums, a small percentage of the fry can be started out with microscopic food.

Trichopsis—Croaking Gouramis

The Croaking Gouramis of the small genus *Trichopsis* occupy an interesting place in the Anabantoid aquarium hobby. They are more easily available than many of the other small, slender-bodied Gouramis, largely because they share the adaptability of the more common Gouramis *(Trichogaster* and *Colisa)*. At the same time, they occupy a similar ecological niche to the extremely delicate (and therefore rare) Licorice Gourami group. A *Trichopsis* tank can offer a fascinating spectacle, all the while providing an aquarist with fish-keeping experience at the entry level for the keeping of some very rare species.

Trichopsis is a bit of a mess as a genus. It is a grouping that truly challenges scientists' concept of what a species is. These fish occur across a number of islands and very rugged terrain. This would be expected to lead to the long-term reproductive isolation of populations. When this happens with most fish, the usual result is an explosion of species, each with a limited geo-

The Kissing Gourami (Helostoma teminicki).

graphic range. Whether this phenomenon has lead to the development of new *Trichopsis* species is a debate in specialist circles. Apparently, *Trichopsis* species can often interbreed and produce fertile fry. However, many of these fish would never encounter each other in the wild. Therefore, the value of crossbreeding experiments in the artificial environment of the aquarium can be, and is, questioned. At the moment, pending future study, apparently three valid species of Croaking Gouramis exist.

The label of "Croaking" Gouramis has nothing to do with their hardiness! These fish sing when kept in clean, often-changed water with good filtration. Displaying males will often get vocal, producing squeaking and croaking noises. They will never replace canaries in either volume or musical ability, but they are interesting.

Trichopsis vittata
(Cuvier and Valenciennes, 1831)

This small, 2.5-inch (7-cm) fish usually travels under the trade name of the Croaking Gourami. It cannot be considered a common fish. However, it does make occasional appearances in the pet stores of larger centers. With a little work, and maybe a special order at a favorite aquarium shop, it can be found.

T. vittata has a wide geographic range, living in rice fields, slow streams, ponds, ditches, canals, forests, and the crowded cities of Vietnam, Indonesia, Malaysia, Thailand, and Eastern India. As is usually the case with small fish that colonize microhabitats over a large range, this little survivor has many geographic varieties. Coloration may vary, but all share the same body shape and a large dark patch above and behind the gills.

Young adults can be very hard to sex. By holding female fish up to a very bright light, a sharp-eyed aquarist can sometimes discern either a yellowish or dark triangular shape at the rear of the body cavity, under the swim bladder. This is the ovary. Since the average busy aquarium shop will not look kindly upon such activities, people intending to breed any *Trichopsis* species would be advised to purchase at least half a dozen specimens and make pairs based upon behavior.

Breeding *T. vittata* is interesting, as their spawning behavior reflects their great adaptability. They prefer to build their bubble nests under floating leaves. In a pinch, though, they will even build surface nests or nests in crevices closer to the bottom of the tank. They will make use of the conditions at hand. The young are capable of eating baby brine shrimps as soon as they are free-swimming, at approximately four days of age.

Trichopsis schalleri
(Ladiges 1962)

Schalleri's Croaking Gouramis (or Croaking Gouramis) are a close relative of both *T. vittata* and *T. pumila* and can interbreed with both. They could be seen as a missing link in a puzzle few are working on at the point of writing. Whatever their taxonomic status, they are an interesting and attractive species. These fish have paler colors and more light reddish brown and blue than most populations of *T. vittata*. *T. schalleri* can look like larger versions of *T. pumila*. Interestingly, these fish share habitats with *T. vittata* in Thailand and do not seem to interbreed in the wild. In aquariums, when given no choice of mates, viable hybrid fry can be produced.

T. schalleri are kept in the same way as *T. vittata*, at a temperature in the mid-70s°F (mid-20s°C). Their tank should be in a quiet place, as they are easily frightened.

Trichopsis pumila
(Arnold 1936)

Trichopsis pumila, the Pygmy Croaking Gourami, is probably the most interesting fish in its group. Its distinction is its size. This Gourami from Cambodia, Thailand, the Malay Peninsula, and possibly Sumatra tops out at 1.5 inches (3.5 cm) but often remains smaller. This can make it a problematic fish for the community aquarium, as larger fish may attempt to eat or harass it. However, in a community of small fish, it is an absolute gem. It is a perky little species.

T. pumila is oriented toward the bottom of the tank. Although its colors in the pet shop may not make anyone look twice (pale brown, pale red, and light blue), its magnificent blue-green eyes in a shady, planted tank will glow from across the average room. Its reflective abilities are striking. Its body coloration is also quite reflective, especially as it cruises out of shadows.

Adult males have longer dorsal and anal fins than females, although younger fish are as hard to sex as other *Trichopsis* species. If the hobbyist establishes a pair in a tank, he or she will observe some interesting spawning behavior. Although the fish will build bubble nests under the surface under leaves, it also has a pronounced tendency to nest in caves under pieces of driftwood and under low, broad-leaved plants. Gouramis that choose a bright green leaf as a roof to their nests are of special interest to curious fish keepers. Observing egg and fry development against such a background is much easier than when against the glare at the surface of most aquariums. Pygmy Croaking Gourami fry are smaller than the other *Trichopsis* species and need microscopic or liquid fry food to start.

Like other *Trichopsis,* this fish does not lay one egg at a time but produces packets of half a dozen eggs at a time. This interesting adaptation sometimes allows *Trichopsis pumila* to move eggs around and maintain more than one nest. This secretive little fish does not necessarily spawn under the nest as other Gouramis do.

Parosphromenus—Licorice Gouramis

So much is still to be learned about the Licorice Gourami group. As if to tempt people into approaching the puzzle, these mysterious little Anabantoids have beautiful colors and fascinating behavior. For an aquarist who wants to break new ground, this is a wide-open area. These rain forest gems are well worth the trouble involved in learning how to keep, find, and breed them.

Work being done by aquarists should make these tiny beauties more available, as the mysteries and myths surrounding their keeping are slowly being replaced by tested information. In this sense, they are very much like the small, bubble-nesting, wine-red Betta species. The aquarium keeper's cliché is that fish like Licorice Gouramis die if someone coughs in the next room. They are rumored to be supremely delicate, short-lived, and troublesome. None of these myths are holding, as these animals are finally being exported. Aquarists have established that these fish will breed for up to three years, that several species can be maintained (if not bred) in water of moderate hardness, and that some species can live in unheated aquariums. In many ways, their position in the hobby is like that of South America's *Apistogramma* Dwarf Cichlids—long rumored to be impossible to keep but now commonly available in larger pet stores as a result of aquarists learning to meet their needs.

Parosphromenus deissneri
(Bleeker 1859)

Deissner's Licorice Gourami is the only member of its group to appear in most larger aquarium books simply because it was the first of the group described. It is only slightly easier to find than the other Licorice group members, but it is just as interesting. It comes in a variety of wild color forms and may well turn out to be more than one species. The recent description of the *P. deissneri*–like *Parosphromenus bintan* (Kottelat and Ng 1998) is an interesting development in this area.

This diminutive, 1.5-inch (4-cm) fish originates in Malaysia, Sumatra, and Singapore, where it generally inhabits shallow, slow-moving streams. It is found in extremely clean, tannin-stained water, often under overhanging shoreline vegetation, in leaf litter, or in weedy shallows where streams have overflowed their

The Croaking Gourami (Trichopsis vittata).

Parosphromenus linkei.

The Dwarf Croaking Gourami (Trichopsis pumila).

Parosphromenus deissneri.

Schaller's Croaking Gourami (Trichopsis schalleri).

Parosphromenus allani.

Parosphromenus anjunganensis.

Parosphromenus nagyi.

Parosphromenus harveyi.

Parosphromenus paludicola.

Parosphromenus *sp.* "Red."

Parosphromenus sp. *"Blue line."*

Several Parosphromenus Species

Species Name	Describer	Geographic Origin	Details
P. allani	Brown 1987	Sarawak and Borneo	A lovely, vividly colored species.
P. anjunganensis	Kottelat 1991	Kalimantan and Borneo	
P. filamentosus	Vierke 1981	Southeastern Borneo	A relatively hardy Licorice Gourami with a spear-shaped caudal fin on both sexes.
P. harveyi	Brown 1988	Western Malaysia	A P. deissneri–like species.
P. linkei	Kottelat 1991	Kalimantan	It features a distinctive side blotch and is not as colorful as its relatives. It is shy and has been successfully kept at temperatures in the low 70s°F (20s°C). Species members are skilled jumpers.
P. nagyi	Schaller 1985	Eastern Malaysia	A spectacular, blue-colored species.
P. ornaticauda	Kottelat 1991	Western Kalimantan	A small species even for Licorice Gouramis, 1 inch (2.5 cm) in length. Magnificently colored.
P. paludicola	Tweedie 1952	Malaysia and Thailand	A delicate member of the group.
P. parvulus	Vierke 1979	Southern Borneo	A less colorful Licorice Gourami.

banks. The standard technique for capturing these cautious animals is to scoop out the leaves they are hiding in and then start sorting.

P. deissneri can be kept in moderately soft water. The authors have had specimens live for two years in medium hard, pH 7.4, dechlorinated tap water in a heavily planted community tank with West African Lampeye Killies. The Licorice Gouramis did not spawn under such conditions. However, when transferred to their own species tank, with very soft and acidic water, they not only spawned but raised their small brood of fry successfully. The breeding tank should be shaded to dark (room light will do) and be in the 80°F (26°C) range. As befits Anabantoids from habitats with a current, however minimal, they do not build floating surface nests. Their bubble nests are constructed under leaves near the bottom or in caves. The eggs are slightly adhesive. The fry need microscopic food to start but are not difficult to raise if their need for clean water is respected.

P. deissneri, like other Licorice Gouramis, are a Labyrinth Fish with no overwhelming need for their air-breathing apparatus. These fish can live underwater with no access to the surface, as they have evolved in relatively oxygen-rich water.

Why do these fish have such a difficult reputation? To begin, they seem to ship badly. Losses are often experienced soon after purchase, while fish that survive the crucial first few weeks in a tank will generally prosper afterward. They are also easily intimidated and need shading and hiding places to show any kind of coloration. They are not good community tank candidates due to their timidity. However, they do well with small Rasbora species and can coexist well with the tiny African *Neolebias* Tetra species or with small surface-oriented Killifish or Rice Fish.

They are also difficult to feed. They will eat high-quality frozen food as long as the pieces are small enough for their mouths. Flake is eventually accepted if they are in a community with hungry Tetras or Rasboras to show them flakes are edible. They are not naturally attracted to food that does not swim. The easiest diet is a combination of freshly hatched baby brine shrimps, *Daphnia* or *Grindal,* or white worms. Live food tends to be the domain of experienced aquarists, however. Keeping Licorice Gouramis is not a project likely to appeal to newcomers to the hobby.

The other *Parosphromenus* species, described or not, are quite similar in their needs and sizes. The table describes them briefly.

As would be expected with a group of fish that has only recently drawn the attention of not only aquarists but also of the scientific community, a number of color varieties and undescribed species are appearing in the aquarium trade. *P. deissneri,* for example, comes in blue and red forms. Wholesale lists include *Parosphromenus* with trade names like "blue line" or "red line," or in lucky cases with geographic place names attached (the radiantly colored *P.* sp. *sukamara* or the more modest *P.* sp. *palangkaraya*). Given the great difficulties in identifying and telling apart Licorice Gouramis, information on where they come from can be almost as useful as looking up the original descriptions in helping a hobbyist make an educated guess as to which of these beautiful Anabantoids he or she is looking at. Finding a store tank of Licorice Gouramis with no species name and no location of origin information will give the Gourami keeper some wonderful fish but also an extremely difficult task if that person wants to identify the particular species.

Pseudosphromenus— Spiketail Gouramis

The Spiketail Gouramis are really surprising fish. Although many slender-bodied Anabantoids have gone in the direction of ecological specialization, Spiketails get along with any reasonable tank mates or environmental conditions. They are survivors, not only in the wild but also in the tanks of inexperienced Gourami keepers. Anyone who enjoys keeping Dwarf Gouramis *(Colisa)* will appreciate the attractions of Spiketails. *Pseudosphromenus* are not the most colorful of Gouramis, but they are attractive. They are seen occasionally at best but are a fish that can generally be ordered by aquarium stores.

The authors have seen battered specimens arrive in states of bad health no other Gourami would recover from. Yet these shake off infections and recover within a week of being kept in unmedicated, clean aquariums.

Pseudophromenus cupanus.

The Spiketail Gourami (**Pseudophromenus dayi**).

Pseudosphromenus cupanus
(Cuvier and Valenciennes 1831)

The fact this little, 2.5-inch (6-cm) Gourami was described in the scientific literature as early as 1831 should be a giveaway. It, like many tropical fish studied at that time, is a coastal species. The Spiketailed Gourami comes from southeast India and along the coast of Sri Lanka. As a generalization, it is found in water—fresh, brackish, warm, or cool. Spiketails like slow-moving water of all types. In highland streams, they live at 60°F (16°C). In shallow lowland

habitats, their environments can heat up to the low 90s°F (low to mid-30s°C). In Gourami terms, they are the definition of adaptable.

Getting them to spawn is not difficult, as they can be conditioned on almost all commonly available fish foods. Sexing young fish can be a challenge. However, just like many other aquarium fish, females are rounder if viewed from above. If a pair is found (purchasing a small group of six will help increase the hobbyist's chances), they will construct bubble nests for their sinking eggs under floating plants at the surface, under overhanging leaves, in caves, or under bogwood deeper in the aquarium. Raising fry can be hard, as the fish are easily spooked by tank mates or human activities around the tank. For breeding, a single-species tank in a quiet spot is recommended. The fry are small and need microorganisms or extremely small food to make it to the point where they can handle the usual fry foods.

While Gourami brood care is usually the domain of the male, Spiketails remain forever practical about the business of survival. Females will sometimes join in the work. The fish will also occasionally have two bubble nests and transfer fry.

Pseudosphromenus dayi
(Kohler 1909)

The Red Spiketail comes from western India. It is distinguished from *P. cupanus* by its slightly larger size of 3 inches (8 cm), its extended tail spike, and its relatively more slender body. These fish offer the aquarist one major advantage over *P. cupanus*—the sexes are easy to tell apart. Males have pointed dorsal and anal fins, and their caudal spike is longer than the more rounded fins of the female. However, their trade

Malpulutta kretseri.

name of the Red Spiketail is deceptive. That color is not always present in *P. dayi*, but it can appear on *P. cupanus*.

Malpulutta

This is a single-species genus.

Malpulutta kretseri

(Deraniyagala 1937)

On the basis of superficial appearance, lumping this fish in with the Spiketail Gouramis of the *Pseudosphromenus* group would be tempting. However, for the aquarist interested in keeping them, this would be disastrous. In comparison with the hardy Spiketails, *Malpulutta* are a delicate, difficult fish for the specialist. They are extremely interesting but very rarely seen in aquariums. Indeed, even in the wild, they are hard to capture. A good part of their known range in Sri Lanka has recently become a wildlife refuge, so future large-scale commercial imports are unlikely. The survival of this species in the aquarium hobby will depend upon the skill and motivation of individuals lucky enough to find the

fish and breed it. At the moment, it would seem to be disappearing from aquariums.

Male *Malpulutta kretseri* grow to a maximum of 3.5 inches (9 cm), while females are much smaller. It is a cave-spawning bubble nester that likes to nest close to the substrate. Broods are small and need consistently clean, soft water if they are to survive to adulthood.

Although *Malpulutta* are attractively colored, with a nice shade of baby blue on their fin edges, they are also well camouflaged. Their secretive ways would hurt their popularity even if they were commonly available, as they tend to hover under leaves. In spite of this, they remain a very sought-after, desirable fish.

Sphaerichthys—Chocolate Gouramis

The Chocolate Gouramis occupy a very unexpected niche in the aquarium hobby. On one hand, all of these species should be rare, given their black-water origins, their somewhat drab coloration, and the fact they are mouthbrooders. Yet, at least one species of Chocolate

***The Chocolate Gourami* (Sphaerichthys osphromenoides osphromenoides).**

Gourami is sporadically available in larger pet shops, usually at fairly low prices. When they are imported, they generally sell quickly. Part of their unexpected popularity comes from their long presence in the aquarium literature, which has presented *Sphaerichthys* as a desirable rarity. To many, they are the "Discus" of Gouramis—a true challenge for any ambitious aquarist. The fact that so many continue to work at the rewarding project of keeping and maybe even breeding *Sphaerichthys* is a measure of the Chocolate's shy, discrete beauty.

Sphaerichthys osphromenoides osphromenoides
(Canestrini 1860)

These fish are the Chocolate Gourami of the hobby. They top out at 2 inches (5 cm). Their coloration is subdued yet striking. The overall color is a rich brown with a series of honeyish, cream-colored, vertical stripes. The dorsal fins of males are pointed, while those of females are rounded.

Chocolates have not done well in their relationship with humans. These are fish from warm black water. As such, they do not adapt well to change. Their entire evolution has favored specialization, which has allowed them to populate environments less narrowly adapted animals cannot even enter. It was their bad fortune to live in regions that have seen massive industrial and agricultural development with its attendant ecological degradation. The Singapore populations of this shy beauty may already be extinct. However, the species still flourishes in slowly flowing, densely overgrown, rainwater streams in Malaysia and Sumatra. The fate of the Singaporean Chocolates underlines the dangers faced by all the delicate black-water Gouramis.

Chocolates are best kept in reasonably sized aquariums, in spite of their size, as maintaining stable water conditions for them can be tough. They do very well in shallow planted tanks with very soft, acidic water. They have a certain popularity among aquarium plant aficionados who use carbon dioxide (CO_2) systems in their jungle tanks. They also respond well to peat filtration, part of the overall dimly lit aquarium environment they favor. Chocolates can be kept in large groups. However, they do not prosper in community tanks unless they are kept with equally shy species, like some of the less active and tinier Rasbora species.

Breeding the fish is a coup. These mouthbrooders produce small numbers of young. They release their well-developed young after close to three weeks at temperatures around or slightly above 80°F (27°C). The young will immediately take freshly hatched brine shrimps and grow quickly if the water is kept very clean.

Sphaerichthys osphromenoides selatanensis
(Vierke 1979)

This fish from southeastern Borneo and the "standard" Chocolate Gouramis differ in the fin ray counts and gill cover shape. *Selatanensis* appears to have a more pointed head than its close relative and more vertical striping (along the lateral line and belly). Care is the same for both fish.

Sphaerichthys acrostoma
(Vierke 1979)

This fish carries the popular name of the Giant Chocolate Gourami. In this case, *Giant* is as strange an appellation as *popular,* as this extraordinarily rare fish is only 3.5 inches (9 cm) long. This Chocolate from Borneo is available only in specialist circles and, even then, not often seen.

Sphaerichthys vaillanti
(Pellegrin 1930)
This small, 2-inch (5-cm) Chocolate is another uncommon aquarium fish and may be the most colorful of the group. It comes from Northwestern Borneo. On the extremely rare occasions it is imported, it is sold under the name of the Samurai Chocolate Gourami.

Parasphaerichthys

Parasphaerichthys ocellatus
(Prashad and Mukerji 1929)
At first glance, this tiny testament to the diversity of Gouramis could be mistaken for an oddball live-bearer. However, a closer look shows it to be a chunky-bodied Gourami species. This 1.5-inch (4-cm) mouthbrooder features a beige/caramel base color decorated with dark blotches. The False or Burmese Chocolate Gourami comes from northern Myanmar in the area of Lake Inle. It would seem to be more accepting of moderate water hardness than its relatives. As a species from a mountainous habitat, it seems to tolerate cooler water in the mid-70s°F (low 20s°C). Given the extraordinary rarity of these animals, not a lot is known about aquarium care for these curious fish.

Luciocephalus—Pikehead Gouramis

The Pikehead Gouramis have been a hot potato in Gourami classification, bouncing in and out of the group depending on what characteristics are being looked at. Right now, studies show these odd fish to be close relatives of the Chocolate Gourami group of the genus *Sphaerichthys*. They are also close to the tiny, delicate *Parosphromenus* Licorice Gouramis, all based on the spherical shape of their eggs. So what are these weird Anabantoids?

Luciocephalus pulcher
(Gray 1830)
The one described species in the genus comes from Malaysia and Indonesia. It is a large ambush predator that grows up to 8 inches (20 cm). It is shaped unlike any other fish described within this manual. It is a long, thin-bodied fish built like Gar or a Pike. A prominent feature is its sharp snout and very elastic mouth literally used to inhale and engulf its prey. In its own distinctive fashion, it is a very attractive animal. Its coloration is interesting. The look of a Pike with Gourami feelers is not one an aquarist easily forgets. Were it not so graceful, it would look as if it had been put together from spare parts of totally unrelated fish.

Pikeheads need soft, acidic, and very clean water. They are peaceful among themselves and will spend hours perfectly still, hovering and waiting. What they are waiting for will quickly become apparent if an aquarist attempts to keep them with fish smaller than themselves. Their mouths are deceptively large in a vain attempt to match their appetites. They are fish predators par excellence.

It is here that the pikehead loses its popularity. Some individuals (but not all) can be trained to take pieces of fish or shrimp off a stick if their owner is prepared to spend time

The Crossband Chocolate Gourami
(Sphaerichthys osphromenoides
selatensis).

A female Samurai Chocolate Gourami
(Sphaerichthys vaillanti).

playing puppeteer with their food. In the authors' experience, they will not take inert food off the surface or bottom and are disinclined to eat food as it falls. They need time to stalk their prey, lining it up for a lightning-fast strike. They seem unable to adjust to the quick descent of frozen food from the surface. They are wired to engulf other fish, as well as insects and moving worms. Juvenile specimens will eat aquatic creatures like Daphnia, but even young

A male Samurai Chocolate Gourami
(Sphaerichthys vaillanti).

adults will ignore food of that size. A young, half-grown adult can easily eat three to four adult Guppies in one feeding. Keeping these fish is very hard if one is not prepared or equipped to feed it living fish and insects.

Since this is a black-water fish from very acidic conditions, its immune system is quickly put under great stress in the average aquarium. Acidity in water tends to limit bacterial growth severely, which means that the common pathogens most fish have immunity to can be fatal to Pikeheads. They are delicate in much the same way as are Chocolate Gouramis. However, it gets worse in their case. Most of the small fish available as feeders for a fish like this come from hard, alkaline water and have long been exposed to bacteria that are nothing to them but absolutely unknown to their predator's immune system. Keeping a fish like the Pikehead alive for any length of time can be hard.

Are they desirable subjects for the aquarium? In spite of their difficulty and unpleasant dietary needs, these strange mouthbrooding Labyrinth fish remain extremely elegant, curious subjects for the specialist.

A yawning Pikehead Gourami (**Luciocephalus** *sp.*).

The Pearl Pikehead Gourami (**Luciocephalus** *sp.*).

Luciocephalus Species Pearl

This undescribed animal may turn out to be a new species, although it could be a color form or population of *L. pulcher*. It has yet to be studied, as it has recently arrived in the commercial hobby. Little precise information is available about the location or range of its habitat. Preliminary reports show it to be remarkably similar to *L. pulcher* in its aquarium needs.

The Pikehead Gourami (**Luciocephalus pulcher**).

Ctenops

This genus includes only one known species.

Ctenops nobilis

(McClelland 1845)

Ctenops nobilis sits alone in its genus. However, a close look at this uncommon Gourami and its behavior shows it to be similar to the Pikehead Gouramis *(Luciocephalus)*. This similarity extends to the spiral egg structure of the fish. *Ctenops* are deeper keeled than *Luciocephalus,* but both mouthbrooding fish sport similar color patterns.

Like Pikeheads, *Ctenops* are ambush predators with mouths that can open surprisingly

Ctenops nobilis.

wide. They are more aggressive among themselves than *Luciocephalus* are. *Ctenops* need to be kept in large tanks with a lot of varied hiding places for dominated fish. These hunters from India and Bangladesh do best in large groups. They can do well in moderately hard water, but seem to prefer softer, more acidic conditions. They are delicate, a fact complicated by the bulk and size (4 inches [10 cm]) of the animals.

Acceptable water quality for these unforgiving Gouramis can be hard to maintain. Aquarists starting with soft water will often add small amounts of salt (1 teaspoon per 5 gallons [5 mL per 20 L]) as an antiparasitic. *Ctenops* share one hazard with *Luciocephalus* as they hover constantly, waiting for prey to swim close enough for it to be suddenly engulfed. If that prey (usually insects in the wild but smaller fish in aquariums) carries any type of bacterial or parasitic disease, *Ctenops* may become ill because they have limited resistance.

On the plus side, *Ctenops* will eat high-quality frozen food and are not above searching the substrate for something to eat. When kept in groups, these shallow-water mouthbrooders have an intriguing and entertaining habit. They seem very aware of where their fellow *C. nobilis* are in the tank. When they decide to go to the surface for air, they begin their ascent very slowly. Invariably, another *C. nobilis* will begin to ascend within a split second. Anywhere from two to half a dozen fish will reach the surface to breathe at the same time. It seems that when kept in a group, they never breathe alone. One can speculate this is a defense against predators from above, as each is a decoy for its group mates. Then again, when aquarists have next to no direct experience of keeping a fish, a lot can be speculated. That is half the fun of keeping a fish like *Ctenops nobilis.*

Macropodus

Nowadays, *Macropodus,* or Paradise Fish, have a poor reputation in the aquarium hobby. They are victims of bad press from back in the days before silicone sealant, when most aquariums were too small for them. Are they aggressive? Yes, but less so than most Bettas or many Cichlids. Are they bad community fish? Sometimes, if kept with fish that can be pushed around by fish that range from 3 to 5 inches (8 to 12 cm). Are they beautiful? Yes, very. It is time to take a good look at Paradise fish.

Macropodus opercularis
(Linnaeus 1758)

This is THE Paradise Fish for most aquarists. It caused a sensation in 1869 when it was first imported to France. As it proved easy to breed, it became a fixture in the ornate, wrought-iron framed fishbowls found in many Victorian-era parlors. Like the Goldfish, the Paradise Fish has a long history as an ornamental fish. Why?

Macropodus opercularis are blessed with long fin extensions and strikingly marked orange and blue bodies. At an average size of 4 inches (10 cm) for males (females are smaller with less developed fins), they stand out in their tanks. In an era when an aquarium heater was a candle or small lamp burning under a slate-bottomed tank, Paradise Fish prospered at a temperature range from 50°F to 80°F (10°C to 26°C) and proved able to withstand both higher and slightly lower temperatures. One of the authors has kept this species in an unheated Canadian backyard pond from late spring until early autumn. With three males and two females in a 20-gallon (90-L) pond, two large bubble nests were usually on the surface from the point the daytime temperature reached 70°F (20°C) until just before the impending frost brought the fish in to their winter quarters. This is not something one would expect of a "tropical" fish. However, this species comes from cooler climates in southern China, Vietnam, Korea, Taiwan, and Hainan.

The Paradise Fish aquarium should be well lit and contain floating plants to break up surface-oriented territories and provide hiding places for females. Predictably, room temperatures will suffice. In colder homes, though, the fish will not spawn in winter. Water qualities are secondary. The environment should be clean, but *M. opercularis* will adapt to almost all freshwater parameters. Tank mates should be robust though neither fin nippers (like many Barbs) nor overly territorial species (like many popular Cichlids). Paradise Fish are active and not timid.

Breeding should be in pairs. These bubble nesters are stimulated by the warmer end of their temperature range and can produce large broods. Guarding fry and nests is usually the male's role. However, the female will also sometimes participate. The behavior of these fish can be unpredictable in many aspects. Some are quite peaceful with tank mates, while others are quite belligerent. They show a fair bit of individuality. All will defend their nests. Most will happily share large enough tanks with several broods of growing fry.

Given its long history, especially as a one-time show fish, there has been a lot of selective breeding and inbreeding of this fish. Blue and albino forms are common in the pet trade in some areas, and long-finned forms were once quite the rage. Mass production and inbreeding also brings some unimpressive, washed-out looking specimens onto the market in some regions. In some cases, hybrids have also been produced between *M. opercularis* and *M. concolor*.

Macropodus concolor
(Ahl 1936)

This is the less commonly seen (but sporadically available) Black Paradise Fish. This southern Chinese and Vietnamese fish grows about 0.5 inch (1 cm) larger than *M. opercularis* (to 4.5 inches [11 cm] in males) and is usually grayish in color. When kept warm, it darkens and becomes quite striking. It is a fish with a following among older aquarists, who came to appreciate its subtle beauty in the era before many of the flashier Cichlids were on the market.

M. concolor is kept and bred like *M. opercularis,* although it is best not to leave the parents in with the fry in the breeding tank. As with the other Paradise Fish, freshly swimming fry need to start out on the smallest foods available.

Macropodus chinensis
(Bloch 1790)

M. chinensis, from Korea and eastern China, is not a commonly seen aquarium fish. It has been around the western hobby since 1914 but has made few inroads against its prettier cousins. It is a round-tailed fish, smaller than the other *Macropodus* at 3 inches (8 cm). Traditional wisdom says it is really attractive only in its courtship coloration. However, experience in keeping the animal says it is suffering from comparison with the overwhelming finnage and color of *Macropodus opercularis*. It is

Albino Paradise Fish (**Macropodus opercularis**).

Black Paradise Fish (**Macropodus concolor**).

Belontia signata.

The Combtail Gourami (**Belontia hasselti**).

actually a discretely attractive Paradise Fish that should be better known in the hobby.

Belontia—Combtail Gouramis

These are neither small nor beautiful aquarium fish. In terms of the Gourami group, though, they are extremely interesting. They are often compared with the popular Cichlid group of aquarium fishes, not only because of

their appearance but also because of their behavior.

Belontia signata
(Guenther 1861)

These are the most common Combtail Gourami. They come from Sri Lanka. Their coloration is attractive, if subdued. They grow to under 5 inches (12 cm) but need a large aquarium due to their aggressive nature. They like soft water, lots of hiding places, and warmth

The Climbing Perch (**Anabas testudiens**).

The use of injected dyes in Asia to create "designer fish" like this Giant Gourami (**Osphronemus gorami**) *is viewed by aquarium enthusiasts as a disturbing development.*

(76°F [25°C]). They are hard to sex, with the size of the female as she fills with eggs being the only reliable indicator. However, breeding this bubble nester is worth the trouble. Like Cichlids, *B. signata* care for their brood after the young

*Swamps such as this are the habitats of the Climbing Perch (*Anabas sp.*).*

Many fish farms use nets like this to grow out pond-raised Giant Gouramis.

become free-swimming. Both parents will sometimes watch over the fry for several weeks.

Belontia hasselti
(Cuvier and Valenciennes 1831)

As far as range goes, this is the more common Combtail. It is found in Borneo, Sumatra, and Singapore. In aquariums it is rarer, as its dull coloration combined with its 8-inch (20-cm) size makes it unpopular. It remains an interesting fish for the aquarist with large aquariums.

Anabas—Climbing Perch

The Climbing Perch are neither Perch nor climbers. As far as the Gourami world goes, these big, ungainly, and aggressive food fish are the stuff of mythology. Their known ability to travel short distances overland was expanded, in some early aquarium literature, to an ability to climb trees. While fish fleeing evaporating water holes by traveling overland may sometimes be found crossing the roots of trees, it is very doubtful they would go higher.

Anabas testudineus
(Bloch 1792)

This 10-inch (25-cm) Anabantoid is a marginal candidate for the aquarium. Its coloration varies considerably across its wide geographic range, which is from India north to China. As with many Anabantoids prized as food, their range has been altered by longtime fish farming to the point where their actual origins are almost impossible to trace. *Anabas testudineus*'s colors—variations on gray, green, and brown—and its heavy body have kept it as more of a species for the public aquarium than for the home fish tank.

It will eat any tank mates it can and will also nibble on soft-leaved plants. It is a shy fish that needs cover, from which it launches its attacks on its prey. It can tolerate a fair temperature range (68°F to 85°F [20–28°C]) and breeds by scattering floating eggs. It does not care for young or eggs. Males can be identified by their more pointed anal fin.

Anabas oligolepis
(Bleeker 1855)

The other rarely seen but scientifically described Climbing Perch is *Anabas oligolepis,* the green climbing perch. This 7-inch (18-cm) species is from northeastern India and Bangladesh.

Osphronemus—Giant Gouramis

The Giant Gouramis are a group of four species, only one of which has a consistent presence in the hobby. These popular Asian food fish are marginal as candidates for the aquarium, at best. They grow fast and grow large. They are candidates for owners of mega-aquariums. In a 6-foot (2-m) tank, their charm becomes evident, as these responsive fish become quite tame and make good pets. The problem is they are often sold as very small juveniles to aquarists who have not informed themselves about what they are getting into. Fish that grow to 30 inches (76 cm) with a heavy body and a very productive digestive system will quickly poison themselves in the average tank.

Giant Gouramis are tasty fish that will grow large quickly on a diet of pig manure. They can prosper in polluted water. Importantly, in a hot climate with minimal access to refrigeration, they can use their labyrinth organ to stay alive in next to no water in open-air markets. They are popular throughout southeast Asia, to the point where describing what their original range was is difficult to say.

Although pig manure is (thankfully) an unlikely aquarium food, Giant Gouramis are almost too easy to feed. They like plant-based food in large quantities. They cannot be kept with any aquarium plants. Like Kissing Gouramis, they have been known to chew on the algae-covered leaves of imitation plants.

They are also victims of an unfortunate aquarium industry practice. Although much attention is paid to the selective breeding of fancy forms of fish, Singapore fish farms are known to take a shortcut and inject dyes into fish to increase the marketability of unattractively colored species. Blueberry Tetras and injected fluorescent green or red Glassfish are well-known victims of this process. However, the size of Giant Gouramis has made them a target of this marketing strategy. The flanks of the fish are injected with words, symbols, and other harmful but popular messages. A person can get his or her name injected into the side of an *Osphronemus* in some regions, although why one would take advantage of this cruel possibility is questionable.

Osphronemus goramy
(Lacepede 1802)

This is the common Giant Gourami. In rare cases, it reaches 30 inches (76 cm) in length. Its range is across all of Southeast Asia.

Osphronemus exodon
(Roberts 1994)

The Bucktooth Giant is an odd-looking creature that peaks at 24 inches (60 cm). It comes from southern Laos and the Mekong Delta.

Osphronemus laticlavius
(Roberts 1992)

The Redfin Giant is a 20-inch (50-cm) Gourami from Malaysia and Sumatra.

Osphronemus septemfasciatus
(Roberts 1992)

The fourth Gourami in the group is the seven-stripe Giant, another 20-inch (50-cm) fish. It comes from Sarawak and Kalimantan.

Betta

In the minds of many hobbyists, the word *Betta* refers to one fish, *Betta splendens,* the Siamese Fighting Fish. There is such a rich body of literature on that popular fish it would seem almost superfluous to do more than mention it in a book on Gouramis and other Anabantoids. However, there is much more to Betta than meets the eye of the average aquarist. In reality, there are more than 50 Betta species. Many of them are great aquarium fish, and all of them are quite similar in their needs to Gouramis.

Since the group is so large, it will be broken up into working groups for aquarists. This is not an attempt at a scientific classification but is more a system to make the care (and exploration) of the diverse Betta species easier. Bettas are one of the frontiers of the aquarium hobby. New species are still being found at a slow but steady rate, and aquarists' knowledge of them is still rudimentary.

What is known is that Bettas have the same two nesting strategies as Gouramis: bubble nesting and mouthbrooding. The primary division will be made on that basis and will be followed by dividing the groups into large and small species.

Anton's Betta (Betta antonii) *is very rare in the aquarium hobby.*

The Wine Betta group consists of tiny (standard size: 2 inches [5 cm]), bubble-nesting Anabantoids that are, as the name predicts, generally wine red or darkly colored. These are black-water fish, all of which are uncommon in the hobby as this is being written. However, while saying if fish this delicate will ever become popular is difficult, there has been a noticeable increase in their availability over the past few years. They will always be specialist fish, but several species are sporadically available. All of these tiny fish are beautiful. Some are stunning.

Wine Red Bettas flourish under warm blackwater conditions in tanks with peat-filtered water and lots of plants. The water must be kept clean, as they have the same inability to resist bacterial infections seen in black-water Gouramis. A good filter and heater are a must, as is a tight aquarium top. Not only do small Bettas

need the temperature of the air they breathe to be the same as their water, but they are also prodigious leapers. They can find their way out of holes the aquarist would never believe a fish could fit through. A further behavioral quirk is one they share with the Licorice Gouramis (*Parosphromenus* spp.). They are not aggressive eaters and seem to pause for a split second before striking their food. This gives more opportunistic tank mates the chance literally to steal their food from their jaws. If Wine Bettas are kept with even nonaggressive species (small Characins, Rasbora, and so on), they must be watched closely to be sure they are getting their share of the food. Trying to compensate by overfeeding is not a safe option, given the Bettas' need for extremely clean conditions.

Males of some species can be kept together, though aggression and territoriality varies from

One of the wine Bettas (Betta cf. burdigala) *from Borneo.*

species to species. In a small tank, a pair is recommended. However, groups can live in larger tanks, especially in aquariums with large surface areas. Sparring and even some fighting will occur. However, most of the time, the fish will set their own borders. This will work only if each fish has more than one potential hiding place.

These fish can be bred in either the maintenance tank or in a more efficient, single-species setup. Some species will ignore their fry, which can be raised in with the parents. The big problem in presenting the group is that, with the current state of knowledge, the authors can only generalize about these fish.

Many of these little Bettas are threatened in the wild and serve as a lesson as to why captive maintenance is something people should learn about as quickly as possible. Information coming from Asia shows the peat swamps these

Bettas (and *Parosphromenus* Gouramis) need are shrinking due to human intervention as the land is drained or modified for agriculture. Many secretive wild Betta species with narrow ranges will probably never even be seen, let alone named or studied. Those the aquarists are just getting to know may disappear.

Betta coccina
(Vierke 1979)

This slender-bodied Anabantoid is the classic Wine Red Betta. It is also the most available and best-known species of the group. There is a debate about *B. Coccina* male aggression. Some keepers report the species to be quite peaceful, with only territorial displays at the edges of territories. Others have found males to kill each other even in larger tanks. The experience of the authors has suggested *B.*

Other Uncommon, Small Mouthbrooders

Species Name	Describer	Geographic Origin	Length
Betta albimarginata	Kottelat and Ng 1994	Northern Kalimantan and Borneo	2 inches (5 cm)
Betta channoides	Kottelat and Ng 1994	Central Kalimantan and Borneo	2 inches (5 cm)
Betta dimidiata	Roberts 1989	Kalimantan and Borneo	3 inches (7.5 cm)

A male Betta mouthbrooding eggs.

coccina's reputation as extremely delicate fish may have been based on early reports suggesting males were always peaceful with each other. Like many Bettas, these secretive fish do not always fight in the open but engage in an ongoing guerilla war the hobbyist may not observe in time. Bodies appearing regularly in an attempted *B. coccina* community tank (as they would with the popular *Betta splendens*) were initially blamed on disease. There is another interpretation. It suggests the aggression is not usually fatal in established fish but seems much more damaging when fish are newly arrived and stressed. Established communities do seem to function in some *B. coccina* tanks if the fish survive the initial period. Interestingly, the authors have kept short-finned, mixed-sex groups of *Betta splendens*, which had been raised together, in fairly

Other Blunt-Snouted Bettas

Species Name	Describer	Geographic Origin	Length
Betta macrostoma	Regan 1910	Brunei, Sarawak	6 inches (15 cm)
Betta ocellata	De Beaufort 1933	Tawau	5 inches (13 cm)
Betta patoti	Weber and De Beaufort 1922	Northwestern Borneo	3.5 inches (9 cm)
Betta unimaculata	Popta 1906	Kalimantan and Borneo	6 inches (15 cm)

Other Pointed-Snout Bettas

Species Name	Describer	Geographic Origin	Length
Betta anabantoides	Bleeker 1850	Southeastern Borneo	5 inches (13 cm)
Betta akarensis	Regan 1910	Borneo	4 inches (10 cm)
Betta balunga	Herre 1940	Northern Borneo	5 inches (13 cm)
Betta bellica	Sauvage 1884	Malaysia	4 inches (10 cm)
Betta breviobesus	Tan and Kottelat 1994	Indonesia	3 inches (8 cm)
Betta chini	Ng 1993	Sabah, Borneo	5 inches (13 cm)
Betta chloropharynx	Kottelat and Ng 1994	Bangka, Indonesia	5 inches (13 cm)
Betta edithae	Vierke 1984	Southern Borneo	6 inches (15 cm)
Betta enisae	Kottelat 1995	Kapuas and Northwestern Borneo	6 inches (15 cm)
Betta falx	Tan and Kottelat 1998	Sumatra	2 inches (5 cm)
Betta fusca	Regan 1910	Sumatra and southern tip of Malaysia	4 inches (10 cm)
Betta hipposideros	Kottelat and Ng 1994	Selangor, Malaysia	4 inches (10 cm)
Betta pi	Tan 1998	Thailand	6 inches (15 cm)
Betta climacura	Vierke 1984	Sarawak and Brunei	5 inches (13 cm)
Betta schalleri	Kottelat and Ng 1994	Kalimantan and Borneo	5 inches (13 cm)
Betta picta	Valenciennes 1846	Indonesia	2.5 inches (6 cm)
Betta pinguis	Tan and Kottelat 1998	Indonesia	3 inches (8 cm)
Betta pugnax	Cantor 1850	Malaysia	4 inches (10 cm)
Betta pulchra	Tan and Tan 1996	Johor, Malaysia	4 inches (10 cm)
Betta renata	Tan 1998	Indonesia	4 inches (10 cm)
Betta simplex	Kottelat 1994	Southern Thailand	2.5 inches (6 cm)
Betta spilotogena	Kottelat and Ng 1994	Indonesia	5 inches (13 cm)
Betta taeniata	Regan 1910	Northwest Borneo	3 inches (8 cm)
Betta tomi	Ng and Kottelat 1994	Johor, Malaysia	5 inches (13 cm)
Betta waseri	Krummenacher 1986	Pahang, Malaysia	5 inches (13 cm)

A male Siamese Fighting Fish in opal phase (Betta splendens).

A female Siamese Fighting Fish (Betta splendens).

Betta imbellis.

A male Betta foerschi.

A female Betta foerschi.

Betta prima.

Betta bellica.

Betta falx.

Betta schalleri.

peaceful community tanks as well. *B. coccina* are often kept in small, warm (80°F [26°C]), soft-water tanks. They have been spawned in captivity, sometimes through the use of one of the easiest spawning triggers used by generations of fish keepers. Cooler water is used in a routine change to simulate a rainstorm. The fry are free-swimming halfway through the third day after spawning. They can immediately eat newly hatched brine shrimps, microworms, or soaked powder food.

Betta livida
(Ng and Kottelat 1992)

The Jealous or Green-Eyed Red Betta is a very desirable fish that has only recently begun to appear in the aquarium hobby. Like the Pygmy Croaking Gourami *(T. pumila)*, it has a very reflective eye. This feature, in bright green against a reddish body, makes *B. livida* a fish much sought by Anabantoid aficionados. It comes from Malaysia.

Betta brownorum
(Witte and Schmidt 1993)

This small, pretty, red bubble nester is from Sarawak in Borneo.

Betta burdigala
(Kottelat and Ng 1994)

This lovely red *Betta* distinguishes itself by its aggression. Not only will it fiercely defend territories from other *B. burdigala*, but it will take on other Betta species twice its size.

Betta miniopinna
(Tan and Tan 1994)

This is a smaller species, at 1.5 inches (4 cm). It is from Pulau Bintan, Malaysia.

Betta persephone
(Schaller 1986)

This dark-bodied fish from southern Malaysia, the same size as *B. miniopinna,* makes occasional appearances on Asian exporters' lists. It is not common in the wild, and there are concerns about its habitat disappearing.

Betta rutilans
(Witte and Kottelat 1991)

B. rutilans, from Kalimantan, is an attractive species that shows up occasionally.

Betta tussyae
(Schaller 1985)

Like *B. rutilans,* this Malaysian Betta has a tenuous foothold in the hobby. It is a beautiful little fish.

Large bubble nesters: The story for large bubble nesters is not unlike that of the small ones. Here varying degrees of aggression are encountered. They range from males of Betta splendens being used by gamblers as fighting fish to males of even the same species coexisting. What is clear is that all of these fish are fun to keep. The fact all the information is not yet in on them certainly increases the interest level for all those who like to explore new facets of the hobby.

Betta splendens
(Regan 1910)

As far as the hobby is concerned, this is THE Betta. The Siamese Fighting Fish (originally from Thailand and Cambodia) is an old friend to humans. It is commonly available in brightly colored, long-finned, artificially selected varieties that could never survive in the wild. The genetics and keeping of long-finned *Betta splendens* have had entire books devoted to them.

The wild fish (3 inches [7.5 cm]) is a short-finned torpedo of a fish, quite different from the selected strains. All *B. splendens* are bubble nesters with a well-documented spawning sequence. Males wrap themselves around females prior to transporting eggs to the nest. The male alone guards the eggs, then wrigglers, for up to four days.

Betta imbellis

(Ladiges 1975)

This 2-inch (5-cm) fish would be classed with the small bubble nesters were it not so similar to *Betta splendens*. Indeed, studies involving crosses between *B. imbellis* and *B. splendens* suggest the two may be the same fish. The local popularity of fighting fish has muddied the picture due to transplantations and escapes of fighting/breeding stock and also probable crosses between species (in nature and captivity) that under natural circumstances might have never met. Since more research will be needed to resolve this confusion, *B. imbellis* will be treated as a valid species.

This brilliant blue and red Betta comes from Malaysia, Borneo, and Sumatra. It carries the reputation of being a peaceful Betta, which in turn makes it very sought after. There are, however, contradictory reports about its behavior. It is possible the "bad actors" referred to in the anecdotal hobbyist literature as *B. imbellis* were misidentified young wild-form *B. splendens*. The authors have kept small groups of *B. imbellis* in large planted tanks without so much as a ragged fin appearing.

Betta smaragdina

(Ladiges 1972)

The Emerald Fighter comes from northeastern Thailand, where it fills the same ecological (and cultural) niche as the Siamese Fighter. In size and behavior, it is very much like *B. splendens*. It is established in specialist circles within the aquarium hobby.

Betta simorum

(Tan and Ng 1996)

Less colorful than *Betta Smaragdina* but interesting in its own right is *Betta simorum*. It is a 5-inch (13-cm) fish from Sumatra.

Rare black-water mouthbrooders: Mouthbrooding appears in a number of fish groups, including the popular Cichlids. It is an effective strategy for a fish to adopt. While it reduces the number of eggs and fry that can be tended by the breeders, it greatly increases the survival rates for the young. Also, it allows Anabantoids, be they Chocolate Gourami types or Bettas, to colonize habitats in which bubble nests would break. Many mouthbrooding Bettas inhabit flowing water and cool, oxygen-rich mountain streams. This has a definite effect on their care in aquariums.

The mouthbrooding Bettas are not important fish in the aquarium trade. Like the other new discoveries in the Labyrinth Fish field, they are a group with a lot of potential.

Betta foerschi

(Vierke 1979)

Arguably the most beautiful of the tiny mouthbrooders are *Betta foerschi*, slender-bodied, slightly scrappy, but shy fish from southern Borneo. They grow to 2.5 inches (6 cm). They need a dark tank for their striking colors to come out. The fish are dark blue to red-brown. Males have brilliant gold vertical slashes on their gill plates, while females sport the same striking marking in red.

Betta pi.

Betta simplex.

Betta ocellata.

Barbs on the gills of Ctenopoma.

The Orange Bush Fish (Microctenopoma ansorgii).

Betta strohi

(Schaller and Kottelat 1990)

This fish is remarkably like *B. foerschi*. However, the caudal fin features a distinct spike structure. The fish is also from southern Borneo.

The larger mouthbrooders can be divided into the pointed-snout and blunt-snout groups. This division involves more than just the shape of their noses. The pointed-snout fish come from traditional Betta habitats, often from brownish-tinged, peaty water. The blunt-snouted group are highly desirable rarities from rain forests at higher elevations. They need clear water, not above 76°F (25°C), and are expensive.

Beyond that, they are mysterious fish. Much remains to be learned about them. In fact, there are a number of undescribed species of pointed-snout Bettas.

Betta prima

(Kottelat 1994)

This pointed-snout rarity can serve as an introduction to this very large group. Like the others, it is not brilliantly colored or especially active. It is a quiet species that can hold its own in a community tank but prefers a single-species tank. In a community, brood-caring males can be harassed into losing their mouthful of eggs or larvae. The fry are able to take the standard foods upon release, which occurs at around 10 days at a temperature of 80°F (26°C).

African Bush Fish

Sub-Saharan Africa is the great meeting place of fish life. Its ancient connection with South America gives it a fish fauna similar to Amazonia. However, the proximity of Asia has thrown a historical wild card into its evolutionary game. African Tetras, Killifish, and Cichlids are as interesting and, in some cases, as well-known as their South American counterparts. However, African Labyrinth Fishes are not common animals in the aquarium world.

In part, this is due to the state of the African fish-importing industry, which has never developed to the point reached by its Asian and South American counterparts. Many years of ongoing political instability of the Congo River region have kept exportation at a low level, oriented toward more commercially fashionable Cichlids when a shipment does get out.

In evolutionary terms, the Bush Fish, Anabantoid relatives of Asian Gouramis, are late-comers to the African fish scene. They have never undergone the kind of explosive speciation known among African Cichlids and Killifish. A key to the mystery of why may be found in the fact they share their habitats with Cichlids. In their spread, they have to compete with established and efficient inhabitants of a similar ecological niche. There has never been the kind of explosive development of species, body shapes, and niche exploitation found in Asian Anabantoids, although some species have adapted to competition by developing large eyes and nocturnal feeding strategies.

The Bush Fish are very present in the fauna of the African rain forests. However, their body plans and ecology remain relatively undiversified. In many ways, in terms of how far their evolution has taken them from the basic blueprint, many of these fish species remain primitive and quite reminiscent of the *Anabas* genus of Asia. Like the latter, they are also sometimes referred to as a Climbing Perch.

The Congo River Region Offers the Following Bush Fish

Species Name	Describer	Length	Details
Ctenopoma davidae	Poll 1939	3 inches (8 cm)	
Ctenopoma kingsleyi	Guenther 1896	8 inches (20 cm)	
Ctenopoma maculatum	Thominot 1886	8 inches (20 cm)	Also in Cameroon
Ctenopoma ocellatum	Pellegrin 1899	4 inches (10 cm)	
Ctenopoma pellegrini	Boulenger 1902	6 inches (15 cm)	From the northerly regions
Ctenopoma oxyrhynchum	Boulenger 1902	5 inches (13 cm)	

Nigeria and the Niger Delta Offer the Following Bush Fish

Species Name	Describer	Length	Details
Ctenopoma nebulosum	Norris and Teugels 1990	8 inches (20 cm)	
Ctenopoma nigropannosum	Reichenow 1874	7 inches (18 cm)	Also found in the Congo River basin

Some intriguing and attractive aquarium fish are in the African Bush Fish group. Although they are more commonly found in the European and Asian hobby, they are not unknown in the pet shops of North America. They are not the rarities mouthbrooding Bettas are, for example. They have a long history in the aquarium hobby but have never caught on as mainstream choices.

There are two main groups of these fish, divided by their reproductive strategies. A number of relatively nonterritorial species simply scatter their eggs, with no nest and no brood care. There are also bubble nesters, remarkably like their popular Asian cousins. Male Bush Fish have hooks on their scales, used to grasp spawning females (who have the same structure but not as developed). African Labyrinth Fishes frequently get caught in aquarists' nets, which have to be cut to release them. In this respect, for the aquarist, they are uncomfortably like many South American *Characin* species or *Corydoras* Catfish.

Microctenopoma ansorgii
(Boulenger 1912)

The Orange Bush Fish (or Orange Climbing Perch) is probably the best-known fish in this group. It is relatively small at 3.5 inches (9 cm), attractively colored in a patterning and shading that is not common in tropical aquariums, and peaceful. Like all the *Microctenopoma*, it is a bubble nester. *M. ansorgii* build their nests

Microctenopoma fasciolatum.

Grey Bush Fish (Ctenopoma kingleyae).

Ctenopoma oxyrhynchum.

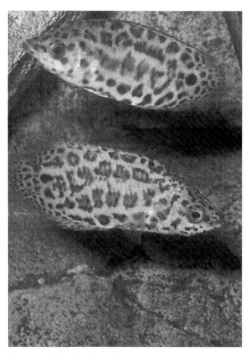

Leopard Bush Fish (Ctenopoma acutirostre).

Ctenopoma ocellatum.

Ctenopoma multispine.

A street-side pet store in Asia selling color-injected Gouramis.

under floating leaves (or under structures provided by the aquarist). Interestingly, although
females of Asian Anabantoid species turn
upside down during egg laying, African
Labyrinth Fishes remain upright as they release
eggs. The male of this Gabon, Congo River
region, species guards the nest and should be
removed once the fry are free-swimming. The
brood care may break down during the four
days the fry must stay in the nest. If so,
although the female should come out right
after spawning, the male will have to be transferred out of the spawning tank.

A tank for these fish should be heavily
planted and well lit at the surface, with fair-
sized areas of shadow along the bottom.
M. ansorgii are masters of camouflage and
can almost disappear from sight if stressed or
frightened. Shade is necessary, as are a lot of
hiding places. The old rule that territorial fish
need to know they have hiding places if the
aquarist does not want them to hide all the
time applies to all the Bush Fish. So does the
rule that if one wants to see attractive coloration (and this fish is beautiful), the fish
keeper must prioritize offering a proper environment to these fish. These are shy animals.

Purchasing these fish can be problematic.
Young specimens are desirable, as full-grown
M. ansorgii have a difficult time acclimatizing
to aquarium conditions. Large, wild-caught
Orange Bush Fish are in that class of Anabantoid known in the retail trade as ich magnets.
Specimens between 1 to 2 inches (3 to 5 cm)
are the best bet. In an aquarium of 77°F (25°C)
or slightly higher, ideally with very clean, soft
water, they should do well. They cannot be
described as community fish due to their

Other Regions Offer These Bush Fish

Species Name	Describer	Length	Details
Ctenopoma garuanum	Ahl 1927	2.5 inches (6 cm)	From Cameroon
Ctenopoma riggenbachi	Ahl 1927	3.5 inches (9 cm)	From Cameroon
Ctenopoma ctenotis	Boulenger 1920	3 inches (7.5 cm)	From Central Africa, the upper Zambezi, and the Congo River region
Ctenopoma machadoi	Fowler 1930	6 inches (15 cm)	From Angola
Ctenopoma miurei	Boulenger 1906	3.5 inches (9 cm)	From Lake Edward and Lake Albert
Ctenopoma petherici	Guenther 1864	7 inches (18 cm)	From Lake Tschad and the White Nile
Ctenopoma togoensis	Ahl 1928	5 inches (13 cm)	From Togo

Rarely Seen Microctenopoma

Species Name	Describer	Length	Details
M. intermedium	Pellegrin 1920	3 inches (8 cm)	Not much is known about this fish.
M. lineatum	Nichols 1923	2.5 inches (6 cm)	The Lake Chad and Congo River basins offer this rarely seen bubble nester.
M. milleri	Norris and Douglas 1991	2 inches (5 cm) maximum	This is a newly described species and is quite small in length. It has no real presence in the aquarium trade. It comes from the lower Congo Basin.
M. nigricans	Norris 1995	3 inches (8 cm)	A rare species from the Congo River region.
M. pekkolai	Rendahl 1935	3 inches (8 cm)	A rare species from the Congo River region.
M. uelense	Norris and Douglas 1995	3 inches (8 cm)	A rare species from the Congo River region.

shyness. However, they can be kept in communities with peaceful fish.

Microctenopoma congicum
(Boulenger 1887)

This Gabon and coastal Zaire fish is of the same size and habits as *M. ansorgii*. It seems to have a greater liking for shadows, spawning in dark areas of the tank. It is not often seen in the aquarium trade.

Microctenopoma damasi
(Poll 1939)

This is a small Bush Fish, with males reaching 2.75 inches (7 cm) and females being marginally smaller. These *Microctenopoma* from the Lake Edward region in and around Uganda do not have a lot of color outside of their spawning period. They can handle a temperature range from the low 70s°F to high 80s°F (20°C to 30°C), with breeding occurring around 80°F (26°C).

Microctenopoma fasciolatum
(Boulenger 1899)

Since they are the same size and with the same needs as *M. ansorgii* and *M. fasciolatum*, they should be a popular Bush Fish. They are pretty blue, gray, and black bubble nesters from deep, clear water in the Congo basin. They become quite tame and responsive,

Fighting male Dwarf Gouramis (Colisa lalia).

Male Paradise Fish of two separate species (Macropodus opercularis *and* M. concolor) *in combat.*

Many aquarium fishes are offered in tanks at the market.

Gouramis and other hardy species are often sold from wash basins.

wiggling at the glass when approached and not trying to escape when routine maintenance obliges the keeper to put a hand into the water. With the right lighting, these uncommon Labyrinth Fishes have striking coloration, with bright blue on a black background. They are in that class of fish that are often overlooked but that quickly make fans of those who do keep them. *M. fasciolatum* is extremely peaceful outside of the spawning period. Males have extensions on their dorsal and anal fins.

Microctenopoma nanum
(Guenther 1896)

The Dwarf Bush Fish is much sought after by aquarists interested in the genus. In color, it resembles *M. fasciolatum,* but its body is much thinner. It stays small at 2.75 inches (7 cm), is a good community candidate, and is not fussy about its water. That is the good news, as this Cameroon and Congo River region fish is difficult to find in pet shops.

Rarely Seen Microctenopoma

There are a number of rarely seen Microctenopoma. They may be common in the wild, but they are not established in aquariums. Usually, this is a direct result of their having developed camouflage over color.

Ctenopoma: There are a lot of egg-scattering *Ctenopoma* Bush Fishes in Africa. All are somewhat closely related. Quite a few of them are good aquarium candidates, generally for hobbyists with large setups. Many of these are food fish in their native habitats, much like Asian Giant and Kissing Gouramis. Most are not very territorial. However, some have a pronounced tendency to barge about the tank with the aggressivity of equally sized Cichlids.

It is doubtful these fish will ever become popular in the hobby. Their size and rowdiness combined with their lack of bright coloration will always cause community fish–oriented aquarists to look elsewhere.

Ctenopoma acutirostre
(Pellegrin 1899)

The Leopard Bush Fish is a neat-looking animal, a fact that gives it marginal popularity in the hobby. Its huge eyes, spotted flanks, and deceptively menacing mouth structure certainly draw attention. However, it uses that mouth to engulf smaller fish. The fact it grows to 7 inches (18 cm) would leave it with a wide range of food choices in the average aquarium.

Ctenopoma multispine
(Peters 1844)

This fish comes from South Africa and grows to 7 inches (18 cm). Size alone makes it an unlikely aquarium candidate. However, its habitat is close to that of a genus of primitive, aggressive, 8-inch (20-cm) Bush Fish that should attract the attention of at least professional or very advanced aquarists.

Ctenopoma argentoventer
(Ahl 1922)

Sold as the Silverbelly Bush Fish on the basis of a tiny silvery patch on young specimens, this is a 6-inch (15-cm) fish from the Niger region. It is an egg scatterer.

Ctenopoma ashbysmithi
(Banister and Bailey 1979)

While its name is curious, this 2-inch (5-cm) egg scatterer from the Congo River region has no hobby presence.

Ctenopoma breviventrale
(Pellegrin 1938)

This egg scatterer has the distinction of being from no fixed address, as the collection location is lost. It reaches 4 inches (10 cm).

Sandelia

The genus **Sandelia** offers two large, unattractive species.

Sandelia capensis
(Cuvier 1829)

The Cape Kurper is an unlikely subject for aquarium keepers due to its aggressiveness as well as its size and appearance.

Sandelia bainsii
(Castelnau 1861)

This relative of *S. capensis* is close to extinction due to the destruction of its narrow habitat.

Conclusion

For the hobbyist as amateur naturalist who wants to learn about aquatic life in all its diversity, Labyrinth Fishes offer amazing possibilities. They also do so for community tank keepers and for those who enjoy breeding their fish. As a group, they offer a contradiction. They are thought of as ordinary aquarium fish. Yet, most of the fish in the group are unknown, not only to hobbyists but even to the scientific world. Sadly, there are fish from this group that people may never know about. Currently, the following species are apparently lost or in danger:

Betta chini
Betta hipposideros
Betta livida
Betta persephone
Betta tomi
Betta burdigala
Betta chloropharynx
Betta macrostoma
Betta miniopinna
Betta spilotogena
Sandelia bainsii
Sphaerichthys osphromenoides (Singapore populations)

One of the wonders of the aquarium hobby is that an individual can start with an interest in a Gourami because of its color or shape in a community tank and take that interest as far as he or she wants to. Keeping Labyrinth Fish can take one all the way to learning about animals aquarists have never seen before and unfortunately may never see again.

INFORMATION

The search for more information on Gouramis and other Labyrinth Fishes can be a rewarding one, but it takes a bit of work. The number of books is limited. The popular aquarium magazines are a good, intermediate source, when they carry articles on these specific groups. The Internet is really the "best show in town" for newcomers and experienced hobbyists alike.

Internet Sites

Generally, the more common *Trichogaster* and *Colisa* species will be discussed on general aquarium sites on the Internet and in good introductory aquarium books. Details about keeping the less common species will be found in a surprisingly wide variety of sources. While it's tempting to offer a list of likely Internet sites, a good search engine will probably offer you more. Internet sites run by knowledgeable individuals may be the best source, but the time demands and costs of running such a site can cause those sites to disappear almost as quickly as they emerge. This is unfortunate, as aquarist-run sites are at the cutting edge of Gourami-keeping information. Perhaps the best strategy is to start with constantly updated, or long-established sites like those listed below:

http://www.fishbase.org (a scientific site which often offers useful wild habitat information).

http://www.fishlinkcentral.com (an aquarium "clearing house" site offering links to other sites).

Books

Rely on your local pet shop for the books you will need. The nearest pet shop is likely to be your most trustworthy source for equipment, advice, and for your Gouramis and other species as well. Other good resources for books and book information are:

http://www.barronseduc.com/pets-fish.html

http://www.finleyaquaticbooks.com (mail-order aquarium books)

http://www.seahorses.com (mail-order aquarium books)

Some of the books you should look for are:
Goldstein, R. J., *Bettas, A Complete Pet Owner's Manual,* Barron's Educational Series, Inc., Hauppauge, N.Y. 2001.
Linke, H., *Labyrinth Fish, The Bubble-Nest Builders,* Tetra (Division of Warner Lambert) Morris Plains, N.J. 1991.
Pinter, H., *Labyrinth Fish,* Barron's Educational Series, Inc., Hauppauge, N.Y. 1984.

If there is an aquarium club near you, becoming a member could turn into a very wise move on your part. Your local aquarium club can be an excellent resource for advice and information from the experienced aquarists you will get to meet. There are also clubs specializing in Anabantoid species. You might want to join such a club, largely to profit from the information in their journals. If this idea appeals to you, try:

The Anabantoid Association of Great Britain
(http://www.cfkc.demon.co.uk/club/aagb.htm)

The International Anabantoid Association
*(http://www.geocities.com/rainforest/andes/
9785)*

There is an ever-expanding, quite dynamic series of small Internet mailing lists available on the Yahoo club sites. In the near future, "chat" lists of this kind will probably develop into a first-rate source of discussions on all aspects of Gourami keeping.

Aquarium Magazines
Tropical Fish Hobbyist
TFH Publications, Inc.
211 West Sylvania Avenue
Neptune, NJ 07753
U.S.A.

Aquarium Fish
Fancy Publications, Inc.
P.O. Box 6050,
Mission Viejo, CA 92690
U.S.A.

Freshwater and Marine Aquarium
144 West Sierra Madre Boulevard,
Sierra Madre, CA 91024
U.S.A.

*Today's Aquarist—The Better Fishkeeping
   Magazine*
MJ Publications
20 High Street,
Charing Ashford Kent TN27 0HX
England

Important Note
Electrical equipment for aquarium care is described in this book. Please do not fail to read the note below, since otherwise serious accidents could occur.

Water damage from broken glass, over-flowing, or tank leaks cannot always be avoided. Therefore, you should not fail to take out insurance.

Please take special care that neither children nor adults ever eat any aquarium plants. It can result in serious health consequences. Fish medications should always be kept away from children.

Safety Around the Aquarium
Water and electricity can lead to dangerous accidents. Therefore you should make absolutely sure when buying equipment that it is suitable for use in an aquarium.
✔ Every technical device must have the UL sticker on it. These letters give the assurance that the safety of the equipment has been carefully checked by experts and that "with ordinary use" (as the experts say) nothing dangerous can happen.
✔ Always unplug any electrical equipment before you do any cleaning around or in the aquarium.
✔ Never do your own repairs on the aquarium or the equipment if there is something wrong with it. As a matter of safety, all repairs should only be carried out by an expert.

Acknowledgments

The authors would like to thank the following people while absolving them of all responsibility for the content: Horst Linke, Pete Liptrot, Andy Taylor, Stephen Guillot, Laurence Azoulay, Roland Numrich, Mary Frauley, Patrick Yap, and Takehiro Furuya.

Photo Credits

All photos by Oliver Lucanus.

Cover Credits

All covers by Oliver Lucanus.

All inquiries should be addressed to:
Barron's Educational Series, Inc.
250 Wireless Boulevard
Hauppauge, NY 11788
http://www.barronseduc.com

International Standard Book No. 0-7641-2105-7

Library of Congress Catalog Card No. 2002018353

Library of Congress Cataloging-in-Publication Data
Elson, Gary.
  Gouramis and other labyrinth fishes : everything about natural history, purchase, health, care, breeding, and species identification / Gary Elson and Oliver Lucanus.
    p. cm.
  Includes bibliographical references (p.).
  ISBN 0-7641-2105-7
  1. Gourami. 2. Labyrinth fishes. I. Lucanus, Oliver. II. Title

SF458.G65 E38 2002
639.3'77–dc21   2002018353

Printed in Hong Kong
9 8 7 6 5 4 3 2 1